BADGER KS3 RELIGIOUS EDU

CHRISTIAN BELIEFS AND ISSUES

Michael Keene

Badger Publishing

CONTENTS

Unit		Page
1	Why do people believe in God?	4
2	What does it mean to be 'religious'?	6
3	Who are the Christians?	8
4	What do Christians believe about God?	10
5	What do Christians believe about human beings?	12
6	What are prayer and meditation?	14
7	What do Christians believe about life after death?	16
8	Why do people worship God?	18
9	What is Christian worship?	20
10	What are the sacraments?	22
11	What is Holy Communion?	24
12	Christian places of worship	26
13	Infant Baptism	28
14	Believer's Baptism	30
15	Confirmation	32
16	What are the main Christian symbols?	34
17	The soul and the conscience	36
18	The authority of God	38
19	The authority of the Bible	40
20	The authority of Jesus	42
21	The authority of Christian leaders	44
22	Different kinds of truth	46
23	Miracles	48
24	Religion and science – friends or enemies?	50
25	Science and the creation of life	52
26	The Christian response	54
27	Vivisection	56
28	Organ transplantation	58
29	Right and wrong	60
30	How should Christians live their lives?	62

Unit		Page
31	What are human rights?	64
32	Taking responsibility for others	66
33	What are 'ultimate questions'?	68
34	The 'haves' and the 'have-nots'	70
35	Wealth and poverty	72
36	Who cares?	74
37	HIV and AIDS	76
38	Four threats to our planet	78
39	Chief Seattle and Greenpeace	80
40	Three very important words	82
41	Animal-friendly thoughts	84
42	Two very tricky animal issues	86
43	ARC	88
44	Wars, wars and still more wars	90
45	Is the Bible a book of peace?	92
46	Is it peace or is it war?	94
47	Christian workers for world peace	96
48	Religions for Peace	98
49	What is suffering?	100
50	What about evil and suffering?	102
51	Can there be a God if there is suffering?	104
52	How do Christians cope with suffering?	106
53	Is life sacred?	108
54	What is an abortion?	110
55	What do people think about abortion?	112
56	What do Christians believe about sex?	114
57	Growing old	116
58	What is euthanasia?	118
59	Women in the Christian Church	120
60	What is Islamophobia?	122
	Glossary	124

You will find out

- The reasons why many people believe in God.
- What the words 'theism', 'agnosticism' and 'atheism' mean.
- What it means to be a 'humanist'.

In the glossary

Agnostic

Atheist

Bible

Conscience

Free will

Humanist

Miracle

Theist

DOES GOD EXIST?

This is an impossible question to answer, although everyone asks it at some time. For centuries people have looked up into the night sky, gazed at the stars and felt overwhelmed by the vastness surrounding them. They have agreed with the words in the **Bible** in extract A:

A *"The heavens declare the glory of God, the skies proclaim the works of his hands."*

Psalm 19.1

As science discovers more about the universe, the feeling of being overwhelmed by it all increases for many people. We know, for instance, that it takes a single ray of light 15,000,000 light years to travel from one side of the universe to the other – and light travels at 300,000,000 metres a second! Try taking that in! It is equally astonishing to realise that, within this one solar system – and there are many of them – we know of just one place where life certainly exists. That is Planet Earth. People have always found this thought alone quite terrifying [B].

B *"The eternal silence of these infinite spaces terrifies me."*

Blaise Pascal, 17th century mathematician

DOES EVERYONE BELIEVE IN GOD?

People can be divided into:

- **Atheists** – they believe that God does not exist and that to think otherwise is just wishful thinking. The atheist believes that there are too many reasons for not believing in God, e.g. suffering, natural disasters, etc.
- **Agnostics** – they believe that the existence of God cannot be proved either way and, until it can, it is better 'to sit on the fence'. Opinion polls suggest that there are far more agnostics than atheists in the UK.
- **Theists** – believers in God. Opinion polls suggest that 3 out of every 4 people in the UK are theists.

CHECK IT OUT

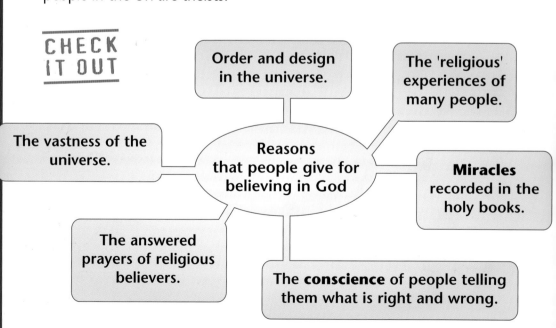

Order and design in the universe.

The 'religious' experiences of many people.

The vastness of the universe.

Reasons that people give for believing in God

Miracles recorded in the holy books.

The answered prayers of religious believers.

The **conscience** of people telling them what is right and wrong.

The tsunami disaster challenged the faith of many religious people.

HUMANISTS AND GOD

Humanists are people who do not believe in God. Instead they believe that all of the goodness and kindness found in this life happen because people are basically good. Human beings treat other people kindly because they know that it is the right and sensible way to live. They do not need to believe in God to do so.

BELIEVING IN GOD WHEN BAD THINGS HAPPEN

Bad things happen to all of us sometimes. When people see events like the tsunami which struck the countries around the Indian Ocean on Boxing Day 2004, killing thousands of people, they wonder whether they can continue to believe in God. Others, though, keep their faith because they believe:

- God may be testing the people's faith. Suffering often leads to acts of great kindness from others.
- Human beings have **free will** and often bring suffering on themselves.
- The actions of God are beyond human understanding.

OVER TO YOU ▶▶▶

1 Give three reasons why many people believe in God. Do these reasons go some way towards convincing you that God exists?

2 Write down three examples of what appears to be order and design in the world of nature.

3 Think of one reason why a person might be:
   a) A theist
   b) An atheist
   c) An agnostic

4 Do you treat other people in a kind way? If so, why?

5 Do you think that human beings are basically good and kind? Give two examples to illustrate your answer.

6 Think of three 'bad' things that you have heard or read about. If you had been involved in each situation, would you have found it difficult/ impossible to continue to believe in God? Explain your answer.

WHAT DOES IT MEAN TO BE 'RELIGIOUS'?

You will find out

- The meaning of the word 'religious'.

- What it means to describe someone as being 'religious'.

- What it means to speak of the 'soul'.

In the glossary

Humanist

Sabbath Day

Soul

Synagogue

Three out of every four people in the world [some 4,500 million people] belong to one of the six major world religions – Christianity, Judaism, Islam, Hinduism, Buddhism or Sikhism. For most people, being 'religious' means that:

- **People are spiritual as well as physical beings.** We know that everyone has a body but religious people believe that they also have a **soul**. In the Christian and Jewish creation stories, for example, God created human beings 'in his own image' and this makes them different from all the animals that God also created. Human beings alone can worship God.

- **Life itself is holy.** All religions have their own holy buildings and places. They have their own holy books and objects that they treat in a special way. Most religions also believe that there is something holy about life itself. Hindus, for example, treat the cow as a holy animal and it is never slaughtered for food. You can see how Jews express their belief that life is holy in extract A.

A “*When the sun sets on a Friday evening I leave behind all the cares of this life. It is the start of the **Sabbath Day** – the most holy day of our week. The mood is set by the Sabbath meal on the Friday evening which I share with all my family. We celebrate together the blessings of family life and our faith in God.*”

Jacob, 17

- **Life has a meaning or purpose.** In everyone's life there are many times when life does not seem to have any purpose. Religious people, however, find that their faith in God helps them to make sense of life and answer some of its most important questions – such as 'Why am I here?' 'Why do people suffer' and 'What happens to me after I die?'

Like other religious people, Muslims believe that prayer is the most important of all spiritual activities.

OVER TO **YOU** ▶▶▶

1 Do you believe that you have a soul? If so, when are you aware of it?

2 Do you think that you are different from animals and, if so, in what way?

3 Have you ever been in a building or place that struck you as being holy in some way? Try to describe the feeling that you had while you were there. Do you think that your feelings had anything to do with God?

4 Write down three important questions that people might turn to their religion to answer.

5 Write down two reasons why either the religious or the humanist approach appeals to you most.

TAKE TIME TO THINK

Imagine that you do not believe in God. Do you think that you would still believe that life has a purpose? What do you think that purpose might be?

Jews regard the Ark in a **synagogue**, where the scrolls of the Scriptures are kept, as being particularly holy.

THE HUMANIST ANSWER

As we saw in unit 1, there are many people who do not believe in God and are not religious. They do not have a religious faith to answer life's most difficult questions. Extract B shows the clear difference between humanists and religious believers.

B *"Humanists think that this world and this life are all that we have. Humanists reject the idea of any supernatural agency [i.e. God] intervening to help or hinder us."*
British Humanist Association

BEING RELIGIOUS AND WAYS OF BEHAVING

Most religions have rules which affect the way that its followers are expected to live from day to day. These rules may cover:

* The clothes they wear.

* The way they use their money.

* The food that they eat.

* The way that they celebrate important events – such as coming-of-age and marriage.

WHO ARE THE CHRISTIANS?

You will find out

- What the 2001 Census tells us about religions in the UK.

- The names of the different Christian denominations.

- Why people believe that there is one Christian Church.

In the glossary

Anglican Church

Baptist Church

Bible

Church

Heaven

Orthodox Church

Protestant Church

Roman Catholic Church

Sin

THE CENSUS TELLS US THAT...

Every 10 years a Census is held in the UK to provide a 'snap-shot' of the life-styles and beliefs of the people who live here. In the last Census, for the first time, people were asked about their religious beliefs. The 2001 Census revealed that:

- 71.8% of the population [41 million people] described themselves as Christian.
- 15.1% said they did not have any religion.
- 7.8% refused to answer the question.
- 5.5% [about 1 in 20 of the population] belonged to religions other than Christianity.

We also know that, in 1950, 90% of British adults owned a Bible and this figure is now down to 65%. In 1970, there were 9.3 million occasional churchgoers and today this is down to 6.6 million. On any Sunday, just over 1 million people attend a **church** service in the UK.

These figures make one thing very clear. Although a large number of people in the UK call themselves Christian, only a small number of them go to church. Most people do not see any connection between the two.

Christians have worshipped in this country church for centuries and the church itself has played a very important role in the lives of the people.

MANY DIFFERENT CHURCHES

For many centuries, there was just one Christian Church. The Church then began to break up into many different churches such as the **Roman Catholic**, the **Orthodox** and various **Protestant Churches** – including the **Anglican Church**. There were two main reasons why this happened:

- Because people liked to worship God in different ways.
- Because people came to believe different things. The **Baptist Church**, for instance, came into existence in the 17th century because many Anglicans decided that people should not be baptised until they came to believe in Jesus as their personal Saviour. Being baptised as a baby, as the Anglican Church did, was not enough.

Today it is thought that there are over 20,000 different Christian Churches or denominations throughout the world. Apart from the larger denominations, there are also hundreds of smaller Independent Churches.

MANY CHURCHES – ONE CHURCH

There may be many different churches but most Christians feel that they belong to the one worldwide Church. This is because all churches have many beliefs in common. In particular, they believe that:

OVER TO **YOU** ▶▶▶

1 Most people would be surprised by the high number of people who call themselves 'Christian'? Did you find it surprising? Give two reasons for your answer.

2 Why do you think that the majority of people in this country who call themselves 'Christian' do not want to go to church? Try to come up with three reasons.

3 Carry out some research of your own to find out how many different churches you have in your area. Make a list of them. It might be a good idea to invite representatives from two or three churches into your school so that you can find out what it is that makes their church different from the others.

4 Describe in a paragraph the beliefs that almost all Christians share.

CHECK IT OUT

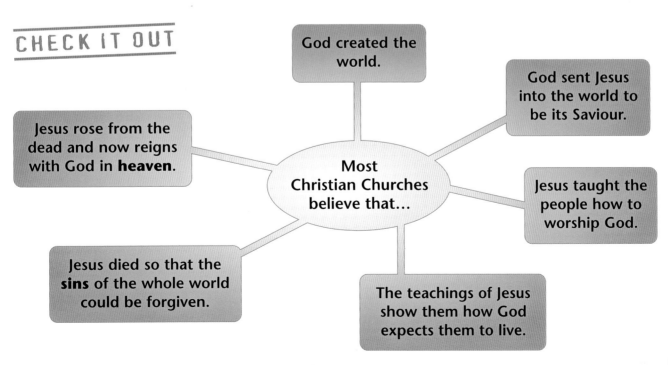

God created the world.

God sent Jesus into the world to be its Saviour.

Jesus rose from the dead and now reigns with God in **heaven**.

Most Christian Churches believe that...

Jesus taught the people how to worship God.

Jesus died so that the **sins** of the whole world could be forgiven.

The teachings of Jesus show them how God expects them to live.

You will find out

- What Christians believe about the Trinity.

- What Christians believe about God the Father.

- What Christians believe about God the Son.

- What Christians believe about God the Holy Spirit.

In the glossary

Ascension

Cross

Heaven

Holy Spirit

Incarnation

New Testament

Resurrection

Sin

Trinity

Virgin Mary

CHECK IT OUT

Omnipotent – the all-powerful Creator of everything that exists.

Omniscient – the Being who knows everything and everyone.

The Judge – the one who decides what happens to us when we die.

Christians believe that God is...

Perfect – the perfectly good and all-loving Being.

Eternal – outside and beyond all space and time.

The Father – the one who cares for us all.

THE TRINITY

Christians believe that God is one but is known to the world [reveals himself] in three different ways – as God the Father; as God the Son and as God the **Holy Spirit**. They call this belief the **Trinity**.

Christians do not pretend that this belief is easy to understand. Many Christians, however, find that water provides them with a helpful illustration. Water can be experienced in one of three different ways:

- as water when it is in liquid form.

- as ice when it is a solid.

- as steam when it is a gas or vapour.

Water, steam and ice are three different forms but they are all water. It is the same with the Christian Trinity. While there are three separate Persons in the Trinity, they remain God-in-one.

In stained-glass windows in churches, the Holy Spirit is usually shown as a dove. This shows that he is the bringer of God's peace into the world.

Christians believe that Jesus died to bring God's forgiveness to the world.

When Christians speak of the Trinity, they are referring to:

- **God the Father.** Jesus called God his Father and encouraged his followers to do the same. This was his way of teaching them that God cared for them and loved them – just as a good human father loves and cares for his children.

- **God the Son.** Christians believe that Jesus was the most complete revelation of God. He was 'God in human flesh'. This belief is called the **Incarnation**. They believe that Jesus was God's Son who was born to the **Virgin Mary** – both fully divine and completely human. This was how he was able to show the people something of God's true nature. While on Earth, Jesus taught the people about God by showing them what he was really like. At the end of his life on Earth, Jesus died on a **cross** so that the sins of the people could be forgiven. Christians believe that God brought Jesus back to life [an event known as the **Resurrection**] before he returned to his Father in heaven [the **Ascension**].

You can find in extract A one of the ways that the **New Testament** describes the death of Jesus.

A *"For God so loved the world that he gave his one and only Son, that whoever believes in him shall not perish but have eternal life."*

John 3.16

- **God the Holy Spirit.** Christians believe that, after Jesus returned to heaven, he sent his Holy Spirit to guide his followers. It is the same Holy Spirit who has continued to guide the Christian Church ever since.

OVER TO **YOU** ▶▶▶

1 Write a sentence about four different beliefs that Christians hold about God.

2 Some Christians find it helpful to think of God as their Mother as well as their Father. How do you think that this might help them?

3 Describe in a paragraph what Christians believe about God the Son – Jesus Christ.

4 Write down two things that Christians believe about the Holy Spirit.

WHAT DO CHRISTIANS BELIEVE ABOUT HUMAN BEINGS?

You will find out

- About the human journey of life.
- The basic differences between human beings and animals.
- What it means to say that human beings are created 'in the image of God'.

In the glossary

Bible

Heaven

Sin

Steward

THE JOURNEY OF LIFE FROM BIRTH TO DEATH

This is the journey that most of us take from birth to death.

The one certain fact in life is that we will all die. Long before that happens, however, most of us will have some experience of death – the death of a pet, the death of a relative, the death of a friend leading, finally, to our own death. These experiences should make us:

- value life as something to be cherished.
- focus on life to decide what we want from it and how we can help others to make the best of their lives.

Some people have their lives threatened by illness and this often makes them determined to enjoy what they have left of it. They want to achieve as much as they can before they die. In 2000, for instance, Jane Tomlinson was told that she only had a few months to live. In the years that followed, she completed the London Marathon, the Great North Run and the London Triathlon. In so doing, she raised £500,000 for charity. In 2006, she announced that she would run across America – again for charity.

Woman to give birth at 63.

Do you think that it is a good idea to have a baby at the age of 63 or not?

TAKE TIME TO THINK

If you found out that you only had a short time to live, how would you want to spend that time?

Only human beings have been given the responsibility of looking after God's beautiful creation.

HUMANS AND ANIMALS

Christians do not believe that animals are the same as human beings. The creation stories in the Bible describe how God created all forms of life first before making the first man and woman. You can see how the Bible describes this in extract A:

> A *So God created man in his own image, in the image of God he created him; male and female he created them.*
>
> Genesis 1.27

You can only draw one conclusion from this. Human beings are more important than animals in God's sight since they are the highest form of creation. They resemble God because they have a spiritual capacity that animals do not have. Human beings alone can worship God. They can reflect on the beauty of God's creation and experience feelings denied to animals.

Of course, there is another side to this. Human beings also carry responsibilities that animals do not have. They are responsible for looking after all parts of God's creation. They are **stewards** – responsible for caring for the creation that God has made.

WHAT DO CHRISTIANS BELIEVE IS SPECIAL ABOUT HUMAN BEINGS?

Go back to the story of creation in Genesis chapters 1 and 2. You can see that the first man and woman had a special relationship with God. Christians believe that this is still the case. Prayer and worship allows human beings to communicate with God.

Christians also point out that God himself came to the Earth as a human being when Jesus was born. God saw how the first human beings had sinned and so he sent Jesus to die so that human beings could be forgiven. Only human beings need God's forgiveness.

OVER TO YOU ▶▶▶

1 What do you hope to get out of your life? Compare your answers with your partner.

2 Draw a map similar to the one above showing the important choices that you have already made and three others that you expect to make in the future.

3 Do you think that human beings are special? If so, in what way?

WHAT ARE PRAYER AND MEDITATION?

You will find out

- The important part prayer plays in a Christian's life.

- The different ways Christians use both private and communal prayer.

- The meaning and importance of meditation as a way of communicating with God.

In the glossary

Bible

Church

Crucifix

Icon

Lord's Prayer

Soul

DIFFERENT WAYS OF PRAYING

In the picture you can see a young Christian who is praying quietly on her own at home. This is how many Christians prefer to pray. They find it easier to speak to God and to listen to God speaking to them when they are alone. Christians also pray, however, when they are worshipping with others in church.

You can also see a picture of someone meditating. This simply means that they are:

- Thinking deeply about God.

- Keeping their mind open so that God is able to speak to them.

When they are meditating, some Christians find it helpful to have an object, such as a **crucifix** or **icon**, in front of them to help them to centre their thoughts. Others prefer to read a passage from the Bible or to listen to a piece of music as they meditate.

Most Christian parents teach their children to pray and read their Bibles from a very early age.

CHRISTIAN PRAYERS

There are many Christian prayers which are very old and are found in different prayer books such as the Book of Common Prayer [Anglican] and the Missal [Roman Catholic]. These are included in many church services. Other prayers are not written down but are made up by the person leading the service – called 'extemporary' prayers. The most important Christian prayer is the **Lord's Prayer** [A], as this is the only prayer that Jesus taught his followers to use:

A **"***Our Father in heaven, hallowed be your name, your kingdom come, your will be done on earth as it is in heaven. Give us today our daily bread. Forgive us our debts, as we have forgiven our debtors. And lead us not into temptation, but deliver us from the evil one.***"**

Matthew 6.9-13

COMMUNICATING WITH GOD

Christians pray because they want to come into contact with God. Why do they feel this need? It is because:

TAKE TIME TO THINK

Do you ever pray? If so, what kind of things do you pray about? Do you think that prayer makes a real difference for yourself and others?

CHECK IT OUT

They have a spiritual part called the soul.

They are able to worship God with all their heart, soul and mind.

It gives their life a deep meaning and purpose.

Why do Christians pray?

God gave them a spiritual dimension.

They are able to bring their problems to God and receive divine help.

OVER TO **YOU** ▶▶▶

1 Why do you think that many Christians prefer to pray to God quietly on their own?

2 Why do you think that most Christians close their eyes as they are praying?

3 Copy the Lord's Prayer into your book. Use different colour pencils to underline:

   – the reminders in the prayer of the greatness and holiness of God.

   – the willingness to accept that God has a purpose for this world.

   – the need to ask God to meet one's basic needs.

   – the need to seek God's forgiveness and to forgive others.

Many people find that meditating is spiritually beneficial.

15

WHAT DO CHRISTIANS BELIEVE ABOUT LIFE AFTER DEATH

You will find out

- The Christian belief in the Resurrection of Jesus and its importance.
- What Christians believe about life after death.

In the glossary

Bible

Cross

Gospel

Heaven

Hell

Miracle

New Testament

Purgatory

Resurrection

Sabbath Day

Soul

THE RESURRECTION OF JESUS

Most Christians believe in a life after death because of the Resurrection of Jesus. They believe that Jesus was put to death by the Romans and that, after three days, God brought him back to life. Christians believe that this was a miracle. It is the most important belief that Christians hold.

According to the four **Gospels** in the New Testament, the body of Jesus was taken down from the cross before sunset on the Friday afternoon. Sunset marked the beginning of the Jewish Sabbath Day. Women followers of Jesus arrived to anoint his body with oil and spices as soon as the Sabbath Day ended – on the Sunday morning. They found that the tomb was empty. You can find out how one woman made the discovery in extract A.

A *"Mary stood crying outside the tomb. While she was still crying she bent over and looked inside the tomb and saw two angels there dressed in white sitting where the body had been... Then she turned round and saw Jesus standing there but she did not know it was Jesus..."*

John 20.11,14

There is one surprising piece of information here. Mary was one of the closest friends of Jesus but she did not recognise him after he had risen from the dead. Clearly there was something different about Jesus but it was the same person.

OVER TO YOU ▶▶▶

1 Here are three passages from the Bible which describe the Resurrection of Jesus:
   a) Matthew 28.1-10
   b) Mark 16.1-8
   c) Luke 24.1-12
   Write down each detail that you can find in these passages about the Resurrection of Jesus.

2 If Jesus did not rise from the dead then, the question is, what happened to his body? Working with your partner, write down all the possible answers.

3 What do Christians believe about:
   a) Judgement?
   b) Heaven?
   c) Hell?

4 Do you think that there is a heaven and a hell? Give some reasons for your answer.

5 "I believe that people make their own heaven and hell in this life on Earth." What do you think the speaker meant? Do you agree with her?

The Resurrection of Jesus took his disciples, and his close friends, completely by surprise.

CHRISTIAN BELIEF IN LIFE AFTER DEATH

Christians believe that the Resurrection of Jesus means that they, too, will share eternal life with Jesus. Jesus himself linked these two events more than once [B and C].

B *"I am the resurrection and the life. He who believes in me will live, even though he dies. And whoever lives and believes in me will never die. Do you believe this?"*

John 11.25

C *"Do not be worried and upset… believe in God and believe also in me. There are many rooms in my Father's house and I am going to prepare a place for you. I would not tell you if this was not so."*

John 14.1.2

Concerning life after death, Christians believe that:

*   They will be judged by Jesus for the way they have lived after they die or when Jesus returns to the Earth. Jesus told them they would be judged on how they have treated others – the most needy such as the hungry, the naked and the prisoner.

*   After judgement, the wicked will be banished from God's presence forever – and this is **hell**.

*   After judgement, the good will spend eternity in heaven – the place where God is. Roman Catholics, however, believe that there is a place of cleansing, called **purgatory**, where the souls of dead people are prepared for heaven.

WHY DO PEOPLE WORSHIP GOD?

You will find out

- The meaning of the word 'worship'.

- The importance that worship has for religious believers.

- The importance of language in religious worship.

In the glossary

Church

Divine Liturgy

Gurdwara

The feelings that religious people have for God are the deepest feelings of all. They may even be deeper than those they have for the closest members of their own family. They express these feelings each time they offer worship to God.

In worship, a person recognises that there is someone of much greater worth than themselves – God. It is these feelings that people express through their worship, whether they are in a church, synagogue, **gurdwara** or temple.

ABOUT RELIGIOUS WORSHIP

Although true worship means far more than the words that people use and the actions they perform, both words and actions are important in worship.

CHECK IT OUT

In worship, people...
- pray together
- sing religious songs
- give offerings to God
- visit holy places
- read holy books
- celebrate festivals together

Religious festivals are very important in all religions. They bring together people with a common purpose – to remember an important religious leader or a significant event from the religious past.

People use the actions of worship, sometimes called rituals, to express their inner spiritual feelings. Singing a religious song together, joining with other believers in prayer or presenting an offering to God all express what believers feel about the world beyond this one – the spiritual world [A]. Usually these actions and words have been hallowed [made holy] by centuries of use.

A *"Jesus said: 'The hour comes and now is here, when the true worshippers shall worship the Father in spirit and in truth; for the Father seeks such to worship him.'"*

John 4.23

THE LANGUAGE OF WORSHIP

People can, and do, express their feelings about God in many different ways. Music, art, mime, special clothes and holy words are all part of the 'language' of worship. Sometimes people get together and draw special comfort and strength from sharing the same beliefs and expressing them in the same way. Sometimes, though, worship is a private act in which people prefer to be alone with their thoughts and prayers. The one thing all acts of worship have in common is that they help the worshipper to think about something or someone outside their ordinary world.

RELIGIOUS PILGRIMAGES

Religious worship is not confined to places of worship. In many religions, worshippers show their devotion to God by travelling to holy places and sites. Making a pilgrimage has been a popular way of showing religious devotion since the 4th century and it still is. Millions of people still travel to Canterbury, Walsingham, Rome, Jerusalem, Makkah and Benares, among other holy places.

OVER TO YOU ▶▶▶

1 Try to describe the deepest feelings that you can ever remember having. What brought them about? You can either talk with your partner about them or try to describe them in your book.

2 Jesus is making an important point about religious worship in extract A. What do you think it is?

3 In the text we say that all worship helps the worshipper 'to think about something or someone outside their ordinary world'. Try to explain, in no more than four sentences, what you think that this means.

4 Find out ten pieces of information about one of the following Christian holy places:

   a) Jerusalem

   b) Walsingham

   c) Rome

   d) Canterbury

The Orthodox service of the **Divine Liturgy** has been celebrated since the 4th century CE and the words have hardly changed.

19

You will find out

- What the key features of Anglican and Roman Catholic worship are.

- What the distinctive characteristics of Nonconformist worship are.

In the glossary

Anglican Church

Bible

Citadel

Holy Communion

Holy Spirit

Mass

Methodist Church

New Testament

Nonconformist Church

Old Testament

Pentecostal Church

Quakers

Roman Catholic Church

Salvation Army

Sermon

Most Christians feel the need to meet together with their fellow believers regularly to worship God. The form that this worship takes, however, varies from Church to Church. To understand this, it is helpful to look at two very different approaches to Christian worship:

ANGLICAN AND ROMAN CATHOLIC WORSHIP

The older Christian denominations, such as the Anglican and Roman Catholic Churches, follow a service which is taken from their own prayer book. Many people feel very comfortable with services based on a prayer book because they have become familiar with the words.

In the Anglican and Roman Catholic Churches, the service of **Holy Communion** is far more important than any other. You will find out more about this service in unit 11.

CHECK IT OUT

readings from the Bible: usually from both the **Old Testament** and the New Testament

the offering: when people make gifts to the work of the church

In most acts of Christian worship, you will find...

prayers: either taken from a prayer book or made up by the person leading the service

the sermon: explaining the meaning of one Bible passage

music: hymns, psalms or modern Christian songs

Salvation Army services are the only ones usually led by a brass band.

Nonconformist worship

Nonconformist Churches, such as Baptist or **Methodist**, do not use a prayer book in their services. They believe that each act of worship should be open to the leading of the Holy Spirit. In Baptist and Methodist churches, the emphasis is very much on hymn-singing, prayers that do not use a set form of words, readings from the Bible and a **sermon**. In a **Salvation Army citadel**, the singing is usually led by a brass band but, in other Nonconformist churches, a music group is more likely to lead the worship.

Two other Nonconformist Churches also have their own distinctive way of worshipping:

Singing, and often dancing, play an important part in Pentecostal services. These services emphasise the importance of people praising God – letting God know how much they love him.

Quaker services are largely silent. People only speak if they believe that the Spirit of God has given them something to say. Otherwise worshippers spend time reflecting and listening to the 'voice within', which they believe to be the voice of God.

In recent years, large Christian festivals, such as Spring Harvest and Greenbelt, have brought young Christians together to worship. These festivals usually last for a week or two. They give Christians the opportunity to worship together. They also give them time to spend learning more about their faith.

Most Catholic services take the form of a **Mass**, a celebration of Holy Communion.

TAKE TIME TO THINK

Christians believe that the whole of their lives should be 'an act of worship'. What do you think they mean by this?

OVER TO **YOU** ▶▶▶

1 Describe two things that you prefer to do as part of a group and two things that you prefer to do on your own.

2 Write down two things that you think Christians gain from worshipping together.

3 a) Describe one thing that makes Nonconformist worship different from that in Anglican or Roman Catholic churches.

   b) Why do Nonconformists choose to worship in this way?

4 With your partner, write down four questions that you would like to ask a Christian to find out more about worship in their Church.

21

You will find out

- What a sacrament is.

- The sacraments recognised by the Roman Catholic and Orthodox Churches.

- The sacraments recognised by Protestant Churches.

In the glossary

Absolution

Anointing the Sick

Baptism

Bishop

Chrismation

Church of England

Confession

Confirmation

Easter

Eucharist

Gospel

Holy Communion

Infant Baptism

Methodist Church

Ordination

Priest

Quakers

Sacrament

Salvation Army

Sin

Viaticum

The word **sacrament** comes from a Latin word meaning 'to make holy'. In most Churches, the most important services are when the sacraments are celebrated. Christians in these Churches believe that the sacraments are the most important way for them to receive God's blessing. In each service, something that is seen – such as bread or water – is used to bring a spiritual blessing to worshippers.

SACRAMENTS IN THE ROMAN CATHOLIC AND ORTHODOX CHURCHES

In the Roman Catholic and Orthodox Churches, there are believed to be seven sacraments. They are:

- **Baptism.** During **Infant Baptism**, water is sprinkled over a baby although, in the Orthodox Church, the baby is immersed in the water. The water is a symbol of the baby's sins being washed away.
- **Confirmation.** During this service, which usually takes place when the person is a teenager, he or she makes special promises to God. The same promises were made by their parents and godparents when they were baptised as a baby. In the Orthodox Church, Baptism and Confirmation take place in the same service – called **Chrismation**.
- **Confession.** Many Christians confess their sins regularly to a **priest**. They must show the priest that they are truly sorry [repentant] for their sins. In return, the priest pronounces **absolution** over them – God's forgiveness. This is most likely to happen before special festivals such as **Easter** and before big spiritual occasions such as Confirmation or **Ordination**.
- **Ordination.** Ordination is the service at which a man becomes a priest. Both the Roman Catholic and the Orthodox Churches only ordain men. During the service, the **bishop** lays his hands on the head of the person being ordained. This shows that the person has received God's blessing for their work ahead.
- **Marriage.** In the Roman Catholic and Orthodox Churches, marriage is a sacrament. It is believed that, through the marriage service, God blesses the man and the woman in a special way. In the Roman Catholic service, rings are exchanged while, in the Orthodox service, the man and the woman wear crowns.
- **Anointing the Sick.** When a person is old, seriously ill or dying, the priest can anoint them with oil. This does not necessarily mean that they will get better. It is intended to prepare them for the journey that they will take through death. The Holy Communion that they take at this time is called the **Viaticum**.
- **Holy Communion.** [also called the **Eucharist**] This is the most important Christian sacrament and it is explained in unit 11.

The confession of sins to God through a priest is an important part of Catholic worship.

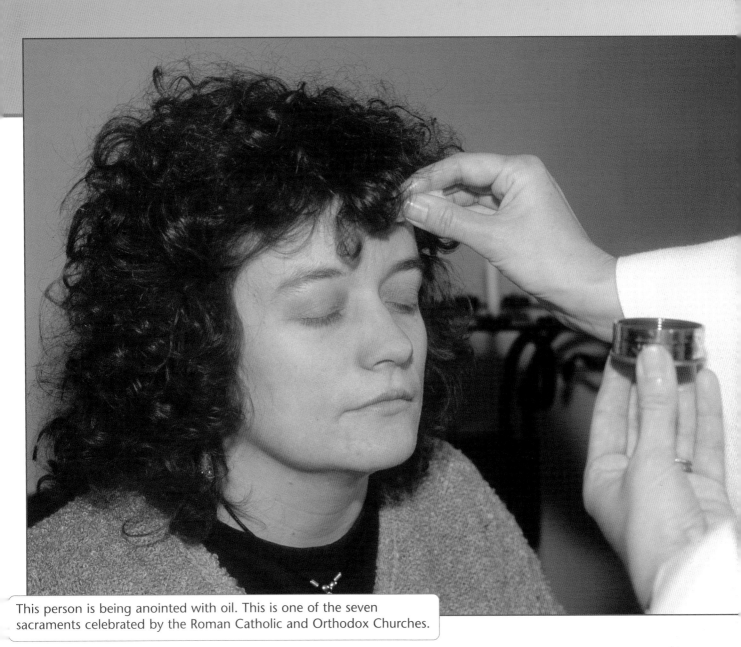

This person is being anointed with oil. This is one of the seven sacraments celebrated by the Roman Catholic and Orthodox Churches.

SACRAMENTS IN THE PROTESTANT CHURCHES

Among the most important Protestant Churches are the **Church of England**, the Baptist and the Methodist Churches. These Churches believe in just two sacraments – Baptism and Holy Communion [the Eucharist]. This is because these two sacraments alone are mentioned in the Gospels. Two Christian Churches, the Salvation Army and the Quakers, do not celebrate any of the sacraments. They believe that the whole of life is a sacrament – that God can be found everywhere and anywhere.

TAKE TIME TO THINK

What do you think the Salvation Army and the Quakers mean when they say that 'the whole of life is a sacrament'?

OVER TO YOU ▶▶▶

1 What is a sacrament?

2 How many sacraments are recognised by the Roman Catholic and Orthodox Churches? What are they?

3 Write two sentences about each of the sacraments except Holy Communion.

4 Explain why:
  a) Protestant Churches only celebrate two sacraments.
  b) The Salvation Army and the Quakers do not celebrate any of the sacraments.

WHAT IS HOLY COMMUNION?

You will find out

- What makes Holy Communion special for Christians.

- The different names given to Holy Communion and their significance.

- What happens during the Catholic Mass.

In the glossary

Anglican Church

Breaking of Bread

Creed

Divine Liturgy

Eucharist

Evangelical

Gospel

Holy Communion

Lord's Supper

Mass

Nonconformist Church

Old Testament

Orthodox Church

Paul

Resurrection

Roman Catholic Church

Sin

Transubstantiation

The most important service for most Christians is the special meal at which they remember the death of Jesus for their sins and his resurrection from the dead. At this service of Holy Communion, worshippers share bread and wine, just as Jesus taught his disciples to do in his last meal with them. This meal was described by **Paul** in one of his letters [A]:

A *"The Lord Jesus, on the night he was betrayed, took bread, and when he had given thanks, he broke it and said, 'This is my body which is for you; do this in remembrance of me.' In the same way, he took the cup, saying 'This cup is the new covenant in my blood, do this, whenever you drink it, in remembrance of me.'"*

1 Corinthians 11.23-25

ONE SERVICE – MANY NAMES

The main Christian Churches have their own names, and ways of understanding, the service of Holy Communion:

- **Roman Catholics call the service the Mass.** They believe that the bread and wine become the actual body and blood of Jesus – a belief called **transubstantiation**. The death of Jesus, by which the sins of all believers are forgiven by God, takes place each time the Mass is celebrated. This service is so important to Catholics that it is celebrated each day in a Catholic church.

- **In the Orthodox Church, the service is called the Divine Liturgy.** The liturgy is an order of service that dates back to the earliest years of the Christian Church. Orthodox Christians trace their service back to the 5th century CE.

- **Anglicans call their service the Eucharist ['thanksgiving'] or Holy Communion.** Some Anglicans share the Catholic view of what happens to the bread and wine. Some others, called **Evangelicals**, hold a similar view to that of Nonconformists [see below].

- **Nonconformist Churches call their celebration of the death and Resurrection of Jesus the Lord's Supper or the Breaking of Bread.** Nonconformists believe that the bread and the wine are symbols. As with all Christian symbols [see unit 16], they are designed to help people to worship God – and no more. They help people to remember the death of Jesus and encourage them to reflect on its meaning.

The Mass is the most important service for all Roman Catholics.

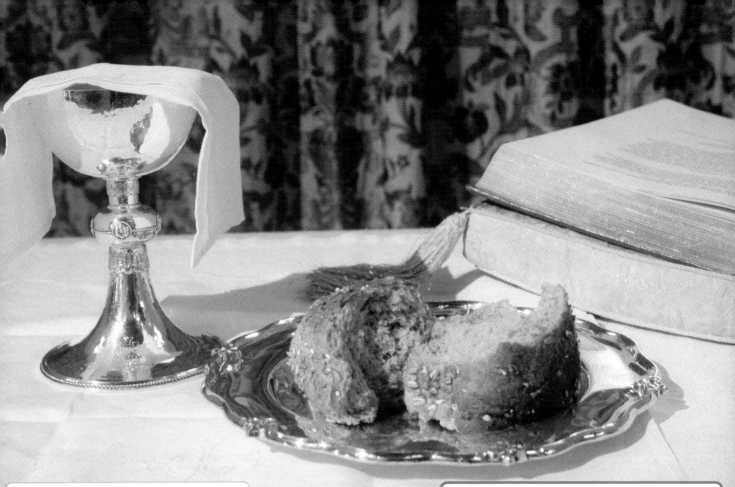

The bread and wine on the table for Holy Communion remind all Christians of the body and blood of Jesus.

TAKE TIME TO THINK

Most Christians agree that the service of Holy Communion is their most important act of worship. Why do you think they disagree, however, over the meaning of the service?

CHECK IT OUT

What happens in a Catholic Mass?

- Old Testament reading
- A reading from the Epistles
- Gospel reading
- General intercessions [prayers for those in need]
- Saying the **Creed**, expressing the joint faith of the worshippers
- The homily [sermon]

OVER TO YOU ▶▶▶

1 a) Draw the two symbols you can see in the photo.

b) Explain underneath why these two symbols are at the heart of the service of Holy Communion.

2 Holy Communion is a 'holy' meal.

a) What kind of occasion might bring people together to eat?

b) How might people make a special effort to share food with others?

c) Describe a meal you have shared with others that you remember. What made the meal special?

d) What makes Holy Communion a special service for most Christians?

3 What is the major difference between the ways that Roman Catholics and Nonconformists understand the service of Holy Communion.

CHRISTIAN PLACES OF WORSHIP

You will find out

- What makes Christian places of worship – cathedrals, churches and chapels – special.

- Some of the differences between the various places of worship.

In the glossary

Altar

Bible

Cathedral

Chapel

Christmas

Church

Easter

Holy Communion

Lectern

Priest

Pulpit

Saint

Sermon

CHURCHES AND CHAPELS

Christians believe that they can worship God anywhere – the open-air, in their own homes and inside special holy buildings. Special buildings set aside for Christian worship are called **cathedrals**, churches or **chapels**. Some churches are centuries old and located at the heart of a village, often surrounded by a graveyard. Other churches are much more modern and found in cities or towns.

Some churches, such as those belonging to the Roman Catholic or Anglican denominations, are highly decorated inside. Chapels, however, are usually much smaller and simpler, without much furniture or decoration.

CHECK IT OUT

Altar or Communion table – found at the eastern end of most churches; the place where the bread and wine of Holy Communion are shared with the people.

Four important features of most churches

Lectern – the ledge on which a Bible is placed to be read during a service.

Pulpit – the place from which the sermon is given.

Stained-glass windows – tell Bible stories or the life of a **saint**.

INSIDE A CHURCH

The focal point inside a Catholic, Anglican and Orthodox church is the altar. This is the holiest part of the building because it is the place where the service of Holy Communion is celebrated – the most important service in these churches. The priest stands either behind or in front of the altar to conduct this service.

In Baptist and Methodist churches, however, the pulpit is the focal point of the building because services are built around the preaching of God's Word – the Bible – and this takes place from the pulpit. This is one of the major differences between the different Christian denominations.

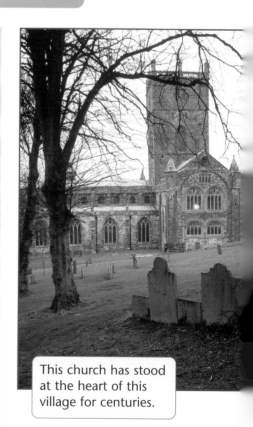

This church has stood at the heart of this village for centuries.

This Catholic church contains an altar and statues of the Virgin Mary.

OVER TO **YOU** ▶▶▶

1 Using 'Check it out' to help you, describe two features that are found in most churches.

2 Why do you think that:
   a) There are many Christians who find it easier to worship God in the open-air surrounded by nature than in a church building.
   b) There are many Christians who need to be in church to feel that they are worshipping God properly.

OTHER USES FOR CHURCH BUILDINGS

Most churches have more than one building on the site – there is usually a Church Hall or a Parish Hall as well. These extra buildings, or the church itself, can be used for different purposes, apart from worship, including:

- Various activities in the local community such as parties, drama productions and other local events.
- Youth groups, mothers' meetings and crèches.
- Musical concerts, both of religious music at such times of the year as **Christmas** and Easter, as well as other musical events.

In recent years, most church buildings have been hired out to people in the community as much as possible to raise money for their upkeep.

TAKE TIME TO THINK

Many churches are now used for 'non-religious' activities. Do you think that this takes away from the 'holiness' of the building?

I go to church as often as I can. The church I attend is beautiful, with many attractive features – lovely windows, a beautiful altar and a very old font. The beautiful building definitely helps me to worship God each Sunday.

I worship in a very drab church building which was put up in the 1950s. All of the seats are moveable and so is the altar and font. There are no stained-glass windows. Somehow it doesn't seem to matter, however, that the building is so unattractive. It is people who make a church anyway.

Write two sentences to explain why you agree or disagree with these two comments.

You will find out

- About the ceremony of Infant Baptism.
- The meaning of Infant Baptism and its importance for many Christians.
- The role played by godparents in the service of Infant Baptism.

In the glossary

Baptism

Baptist Church

Church

Cross

Font

Heaven

Holy Spirit

Infant Baptism

Methodist Church

Priest

Sin

Vicar

In many churches today, the Baptismal font is placed in the middle of the congregation to show that the people are welcoming the baby into the church family.

To Christians, belonging to a church is rather like being part of a family – God's family. When a new baby is born, Christians want to welcome him or her into their church family. In the Baptist Church, they do this by dedicating the baby to God in a special service [called a Dedication service]. In Roman Catholic, Orthodox, Anglican and Methodist Churches, the baby is baptised.

Before a baby is baptised, the child's parents choose godparents from among their friends and relatives. This is an old tradition. Infant Baptism services make it clear that a godparent is expected to look after the spiritual welfare of the child.

I was thrilled when two close friends recently asked me to be one of the godparents of their son. I am a Christian and I try to follow the Christian way of life myself. I will do my best to try to make sure that my godson grows up to follow the teachings of Jesus because I believe that this will make him truly happy.

OVER TO YOU ▶▶▶

1 Were you baptised as a baby?
2 If so, do you know who your godparents are?
3 Have they shown any interest in your 'spiritual welfare'?
4 If you were a godparent, what would you try to do for your godchild?
5 Explain why the parents of the baby being baptised are sometimes handed a lighted candle.

TAKE TIME TO THINK

Do you think that parents should be allowed to have their baby baptised if they do not go to church themselves?

THE BAPTISMAL SERVICE

In an Anglican Baptismal service, the parents, godparents and baby gather with the **vicar** around the **font**, which holds the water for the Baptism. This is traditionally placed just inside the door of the church to remind everyone that the child is being admitted into church membership through Baptism.

The priest asks the parents and godparents a series of questions [see below]. He then uses the water in the font to make the sign of the cross on the baby's forehead before tipping water over its head three times. Why three times? "I baptise you in the name of the Father, the Son and the Holy Spirit."

Questions asked during the Baptismal service

Q. Do you turn to Christ?	A. I turn to Christ.
Q. Do you repent of your sins?	A. I repent of my sins.
Q. Do you renounce evil?	A. I renounce evil.
Q. Do you believe and trust in God?	A. I believe and trust in him.
Q. Do you believe and trust in Jesus Christ who redeemed the world?	A. I believe and trust in him.
Q. Do you believe and trust in his Holy Spirit who gives life to the people of God?	A. I believe and trust in him.

As you might imagine, the different Churches have their own ways of baptising a baby. In some Methodist churches, for example, the parents are handed a lighted candle as the child is told:

I give you this sign, for now you belong to Christ, the light of the world. Let your light shine before men so that they might see your good works and give glory to the Father who is in heaven.

The same thing can also happen in an Anglican church.

This child is being baptised in an Anglican church.

BELIEVER'S BAPTISM

You will find out

- About one Church that only baptises adult believers.

- The differences between Believer's Baptism and Infant Baptism.

- The symbolism behind the service of Believer's Baptism.

In the glossary

Baptism

Baptist Church

Believer's Baptism

Church

Infant Baptism

Minister

Resurrection

Sin

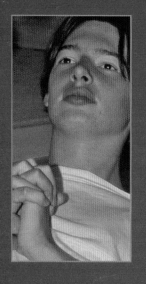

WHAT IS BELIEVER'S BAPTISM?

Believer's Baptism is a particularly important service of spiritual commitment in the Baptist Church, although it is also practised in a few other Churches as well. These Churches cannot understand how a young baby can have faith in God – and they believe that no-one should be baptised without such faith. Baptists argue that it is better to wait for Baptism until a person can make their own decision to follow the Christian way of life.

THE SERVICE OF BELIEVER'S BAPTISM

In the past, the clothes that people wore for Believer's Baptism had a symbolic significance. That symbolism is continued today with men wearing a white shirt and women a white dress for the ceremony. White is the symbol of purity and Baptism is a ceremony to show that a person's sins have been forgiven.

While a Baptism is usually carried out in a pool sunk into the floor at the front of a church, it can be performed in a local river or the sea. Some pilgrims even travel to the Holy Land of Israel to be baptised in the River Jordan – just as Jesus was.

The service in a church begins with the person telling the congregation how they came to believe in Jesus as their Saviour. This forms an essential part of all adult Baptismal services. The person then joins the minister in the water. After announcing that the person is being baptised because of their faith in Jesus, the **minister** rocks them gently backwards until their whole body is beneath the water.

THE SYMBOLISM OF BELIEVER'S BAPTISM

Water is one of the most powerful Christian symbols. It indicates that a person has been washed clean of their sins. There are three important pieces of symbolism in the service of Believer's Baptism:

- As the person goes down into the water, it demonstrates that they are leaving their sinful life behind.
- As the person is beneath the water, they are being 'buried' with Christ, having 'died' for their past sins.
- As the person leaves the pool so they are entering into new life and sharing in the Resurrection of Jesus. Eternal life is just beginning for them and will continue beyond death into eternity.

OVER TO **YOU** ▶▶▶

1   Do you agree that it is better to wait until a person is an adult before they are baptised?

2   If so, at what age do you think a person is old enough to decide whether to become a Christian or not?

3   Draw three drawings to illustrate the three-fold symbolism behind the service of Infant Baptism. Explain in just two sentences under each of them the symbolism behind the act.

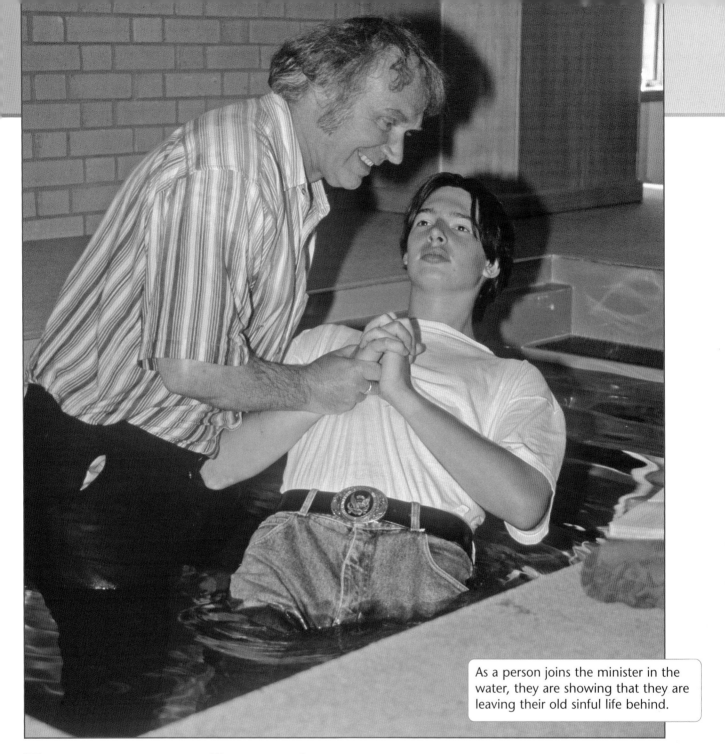

As a person joins the minister in the water, they are showing that they are leaving their old sinful life behind.

THE MEANING OF BELIEVER'S BAPTISM

As you can see, Baptists draw a strong parallel between Believer's Baptism and the death, burial and Resurrection of Jesus. Nothing happens to the person being baptised during the ceremony. No-one is saved or forgiven because they have been baptised. Two things, however, do matter:

- The person has demonstrated in public their own faith in Jesus Christ.
- The person has declared their determination to follow the teachings and the example of Jesus.

TAKE TIME TO THINK

a) Why do you think that symbolism plays such an important part in the service of Believer's Baptism?

b) Why is it important to stress that nothing actually takes place through the Baptism ceremony?

CONFIRMATION

You will find out

- The link between Infant Baptism and Confirmation.

- What happens in the service of Confirmation.

- The importance that Confirmation has for many Christians.

In the glossary

Bishop

Chrismation

Confirmation

Cross

Free Churches

Holy Communion

Holy Spirit

Infant Baptism

Methodist Church

New Testament

Sacrament

Sin

The ceremony of Confirmation is held only in those Churches which practise Infant Baptism – the Roman Catholic and the Anglican Churches. The person to be confirmed can be any age but is most likely to be between the ages of 12 and 18. What really matters is that he or she is old enough to make their own commitment to the Christian life. To do this they make again [confirm] the promises that their parents and godparents made for them when they were baptised. A person can only be confirmed if they have already been baptised.

THE CONFIRMATION SERVICE

In the Anglican and Roman Catholic Churches, the service of Confirmation is almost always carried out by a bishop. He asks each person three questions about their religious faith [A] and these are the same as those that their parents and godparents were asked at the person's Baptism.

A "You have come here to be confirmed. You stand in the presence of God and his Church. With your own mouth and from your heart you must declare your allegiance to Christ and your rejection of all that is evil. Therefore I ask you three questions:
Do you turn to Christ? [Answer: I turn to Christ.]
Do you repent of your sins? [Answer: I repent of my sins.]
Do you renounce evil? [Answer: I renounce evil.]"

The bishop then asks three more questions [B]:

B "Do you believe and trust in God the Father [who made the world]? [Answer: I believe and trust in him.]
Do you believe and trust in Jesus Christ who redeemed mankind? [Answer: I believe and trust in him.]
Do you believe and trust in the Holy Spirit who gives life to the people of God? [Answer: I believe and trust in him.]"

After this, the bishop places his hands on the head of each person – this is called the 'laying on of hands'. This is a very old custom dating back to the New Testament. It is believed to be the means by which the Holy Spirit is given to a person.

The bishop is an important leader in many Churches and his crook is a symbol that he is a shepherd to the people.

This bishop is carrying out an ancient tradition when he lays his hands on each person being confirmed.

In a Roman Catholic Confirmation service, two other things take place:

- The bishop makes the sign of the cross on the forehead of each candidate using holy oil – a symbol of inner healing.
- The bishop slaps the face of each person lightly with two fingers – a sign that all of the sins they have committed since they were baptised have been forgiven by God.

OVER TO **YOU** ▶▶

1 Explain why this service is called Confirmation.
2 a) What do you think is meant by 'inner healing'?
   b) Explain why the bishop slaps the face of each person lightly?
3 Why is Confirmation important to many Christians?
4 What do you think is the value of church members renewing their Christian commitment each year by signing a membership card – as they do in the Methodist Church?

WHY IS CONFIRMATION IMPORTANT?

In the Orthodox Church, Infant Baptism and Confirmation are combined in a single service – called Chrismation. Many **Free Churches** do not have an equivalent to Confirmation although, in the Methodist Church, people renew their commitment to God and their church each year by signing a membership ticket.

For Catholics and Anglicans, however, the service of Confirmation is very important. After people have been confirmed, they are accepted as full members of the Church. This means that they are able to take the sacrament of Holy Communion. Most Christians find that taking this sacrament regularly gives them the strength that they need to follow the Christian way of life.

33

WHAT ARE THE MAIN CHRISTIAN SYMBOLS?

You will find out

- The meaning of the cross as a Christian symbol.

- The importance to Christians of statues of the Virgin Mary and icons.

- The part played by the symbols of water, bread and wine in worship.

In the glossary

Altar

Believer's Baptism

Cross

Crucifix

Divine Liturgy

Eucharist

Holy Communion

Icon

Infant Baptism

Lord's Supper

Mass

Meeting House

Minister

Priest

Quakers

Saint

Salvation Army

Virgin Mary

Symbols can be a powerful way to express meaning and communicate religious truth. Among the most powerful Christian symbols are:

THE CROSS

The cross is the most widely used Christian symbol because Jesus died on a cross. There are statues and pictures of Jesus on the cross in many churches, while some Christians make the 'sign of the cross' on their body as they pass in front of the altar. Some people wear crosses around their neck, called crucifixes.

STATUES AND ICONS

Some Churches use many symbols in their religious worship as they believe that it helps worshippers to concentrate on God. In the Orthodox Church, for example, icons – holy pictures of Jesus, the Virgin Mary, Joseph or other saints – help worshippers to pray. Roman Catholic churches often have statues or images of the Virgin Mary.

Saints are men or women who have dedicated their lives to the service of God. Catholics often light a candle in front of a saint's statue as they say a prayer for themselves or someone else. They believe that the saints are in heaven and able to commend their prayers to God. In particular, Catholics and Orthodox believers believe that they can pray to God through the Virgin Mary as she is the mother of Jesus.

There are many Christians, however, who believe that such statues and paintings are a distraction and so there are few, if any, symbols in their places of worship. One such group is the Quakers. In their places of worship, known as **Meeting Houses**, there is no cross or statue. They do not have a priest or minister to lead their services, which simply provide an opportunity for people to sit quietly and meditate on God.

The Salvation Army is the only Church whose members wear a distinctive uniform.

OVER TO **YOU** ▶▶▶

1 Explain the meaning of:
   a) Icon
   b) The sign of the cross
   c) Crucifix
2 It might seem strange to many people that Christians should choose the symbol of a cross since the cross speaks to many of death, defeat and failure. How would you explain the Christian choice of the cross as their main symbol.
3 Why is water such an important Christian symbol?

Wine is a very important Christian symbol for the death of Jesus.

OTHER CHRISTIAN SYMBOLS

Apart from the cross, there are other important Christian symbols:

- Many churches use the symbolic action of breaking bread and drinking wine to remind them of the time that Jesus shared his last meal with his disciples before he was crucified. In many churches, this service, the most solemn of all for Christians, takes place at the altar. It goes under many different names as you can see in 'Check it out'.

- Water is a very important Christian symbol. It is used to welcome people into the Christian family through Baptism. This service – found in Catholic, Orthodox and Anglican services – is called Infant Baptism. Baptist churches do not baptise babies but only adults who believe in Jesus as their Saviour – a service called Believer's Baptism. You will have found out more about Infant Baptism in unit 13 and Believer's Baptism in unit 14.

- Some Christians use symbols to let people know that they are Christians. Members of the Salvation Army, for instance, wear a distinctive uniform with a badge. Some wear a fish brooch or pin. The fish was a secret symbol used by early Christians during a time of persecution. The Greek word for fish is made up of the letters ICTHUS. These were the first letters of the words 'Jesus Christ, Son of God and Saviour'. Christians understood the meaning of the letters but their enemies did not.

CHECK IT OUT

Different names for Holy Communion

- Eucharist [Anglican]
- Holy Communion [Anglican]
- The Mass [Catholic]
- Divine Liturgy [Orthodox]
- Lord's Supper and Breaking of Bread [Nonconformist]

THE SOUL AND THE CONSCIENCE

You will find out

- What Christians understand by the 'soul'.

- What Christians mean by human beings being made 'in God's image'.

- What Christians believe about the conscience and free will.

In the glossary

Atheist

Bible

Conscience

Free Will

Heaven

Humanist

Soul

Do you know where your brain is? Of course you do. It is in your head. Do you know where your heart is? No problem there. It is in your chest. Do you know where your soul is? Very unlikely – although you might like to think about it for a moment.

TWO THOUGHTS ABOUT THE SOUL

By 'soul' we mean the spiritual centre of a person. There are two different points of view about the soul:

- Many people deny that human beings have a soul. They believe that human beings are little more than a very complicated collection of chemicals working together to produce their muscles, bones and organs. There is nothing else to them!

- Many people, religious and non-religious, believe that there is more to each human being than simply their body. They talk about the soul. They ask, for example, what part of us it is that falls in love or is deeply moved by a beautiful sunset, a piece of music or a painting. What part of each human being is able to appreciate beauty or have the deepest feelings – including feelings for God – if not the soul?

Religious people believe that it is the spiritual part of us, the soul, which makes human beings unique. This is the part of all of us capable of worshipping God – something that animals, no matter how intelligent they might be, cannot do.

CHRISTIANS AND THE SOUL

In the beginning of the Bible there is a story that explains how God created the first man and woman. In this story, two people, called Adam and Eve, are said to have been made 'in the image of God'. Christians understand this to mean that only human beings, among all of the animals, bear a spiritual likeness to God. In other words, they have a soul. This makes them very special.

Christians also believe two other things about the soul:

- Human beings are able to communicate with God through prayer because they are spiritual beings. This is why prayer is such an important spiritual activity for Christians.

- Although the body decays when a person dies, their soul or spirit lives on forever. When a person dies, it is their soul which goes on to be with God in heaven.

TAKE TIME TO THINK

a) What are some of the things that almost all human beings agree to be right and wrong?

b) What are some of the things that human beings disagree about when they consider what is right and wrong?

This young couple are in love but they do not find it easy to explain the feelings they have for each other.

THE CONSCIENCE

Christians believe that, because they have a soul, they also have a conscience. God speaks to them through their conscience and tells them what is right and wrong. Christians speak of God 'guiding' them in this way.

People do not, of course, have to do what their conscience tells them. Everyone has been given free will and this means that they can choose the wrong or an unwise path to take. In other words, they can refuse to listen to God.

People who do not believe in God, whether they call themselves atheists or humanists, agree that human beings have a conscience. They do not believe, however, that it is the voice of God. Instead it is formed by everything that has happened to them, including the advice they have been given by their parents and teachers.

OVER TO **YOU** ▶▶▶

1 What do you understand by the word 'soul'?

2 Do you think that you have a soul? If so, what makes you think this?

3 Describe three things that Christians believe about the soul.

4 "You have to believe in God to have a conscience."

a) Do you agree with this statement?

b) How might a Christian explain their conscience?

c) How might someone who is not a Christian explain their conscience?

5 Do you believe that you have a conscience? If so, where do you think it came from?

THE AUTHORITY OF GOD

You will find out

- What Christians believe about God.

- How Christians communicate with God.

- The authority that God has over each Christian.

In the glossary

Bible

Free Will

Lord's Prayer

Sin

Synagogue

Ten Commandments

Christians believe that all human beings are sinful. This means that they are unreliable and far from perfect. The only perfect being is God and so they turn to him for help and guidance in their everyday lives. For Christians, and most religious people, God is the final authority.

GOD THE FATHER

Jesus left his disciples with a 'model prayer'. Christians today know this as the Lord's Prayer, although some Roman Catholics call it the 'Our Father'. It begins with Jesus teaching his disciples to call God their Father. This was the favourite title that Jesus used for God.

You can read the Lord's Prayer for yourself in Matthew 6.7-13, although you may well know it off by heart already. What, though, did Jesus mean when he taught his disciples to call God their Father? He meant that:

- **God cares for all his children.** If Christians follow the will of God, and do as he tells them in the Bible, then they will be truly happy and satisfied.

- **God has authority over his children.** Human fathers have authority over their children, although the way that this authority is exercised changes as their children grow older. God has authority over all human beings although, at the same time, he gives them freedom to make their own decisions – and their own mistakes!

Christians believe that God has a will and a purpose for each of them. They do need, however, to make contact with God to know what that will is. They do this in three important ways:

1 **Through prayer.** We mentioned the importance of this in unit 16.

2 **Through the experience of worship.** Joining with other Christians in acts of worship helps them to come to know the will of God.

3 **Through the Bible.** Christians believe that God speaks to them through the words of the Bible. This is why reading the Bible plays such an important part in acts of worship and also private devotions. You will find out more about this in unit 19.

The Ten Commandments are so important to all Jews that there is a reminder of them on the wall of every synagogue.

Most Christians believe that it is important to meet with other believers to worship God. In this way they come to know the will of God for their lives.

THE AUTHORITY OF GOD

God does not compel his followers to carry out his will. He gave them free will in the beginning and this still remains true today. A person can know exactly what God wants them to do – and then do something else.

Jews believe that God has made his will plainly known through the **Ten Commandments**. In their earliest days, the Jews entered into a covenant [a solemn agreement] with God and this placed a heavy obligation on them to keep each of the Ten Commandments. Christians today also believe that these laws are important, although they do not attempt to follow all of them.

TAKE TIME TO THINK

Do you think that people should be completely free to decide what is right and wrong for them – or should they look elsewhere for help and guidance. If they need help, where do you think they should look?

OVER TO **YOU** ▶▶▶

1 Look back to unit 4 to refresh your memory on what Christians believe about God. Make your own list of the different things that Christians believe that God can do. Write a paragraph to describe how Christians believe that God is different from themselves.

2 a) Read the Ten Commandments in Exodus 20.1-17.

   b) Try to explain why you think each of them was given in the first place.

   c) If God came up with Ten Commandments for today, what do you think he would include? You can include some of the original commandments in your list if you wish.

THE AUTHORITY OF THE BIBLE

You will find out

- The importance of the Bible for Christians.
- What is in the Bible.
- How Christians make use of the Bible.

In the glossary

Bible

Gospel

Minister

New Testament

Old Testament

Parable

Paul

Priest

Sermon

Soul

THE OLD AND NEW TESTAMENTS

The Christian Bible is divided into two parts:

- **The Old Testament.** The Old Testament is the earliest part of the Christian Bible and contains all the books found in the Jewish Scriptures. The books of the Old Testament cover a time-span of at least 1,000 years and it is not known who wrote many of them. They form the background of much of what is in the New Testament.
- **The New Testament.** This part of the Bible is mainly concerned with Jesus Christ, whose coming into the world was prophesied in the Old Testament.

In the Bible there are many different kinds of writing:

CHECK IT OUT

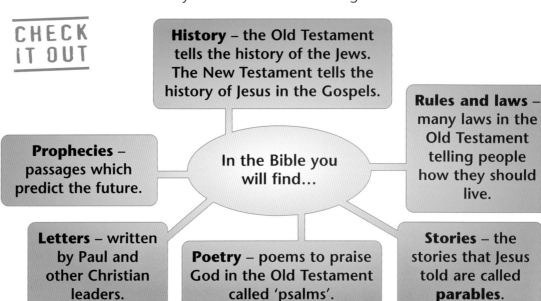

History – the Old Testament tells the history of the Jews. The New Testament tells the history of Jesus in the Gospels.

Rules and laws – many laws in the Old Testament telling people how they should live.

Prophecies – passages which predict the future.

In the Bible you will find...

Letters – written by Paul and other Christian leaders.

Poetry – poems to praise God in the Old Testament called 'psalms'.

Stories – the stories that Jesus told are called **parables**.

WHAT MAKES THE BIBLE SPECIAL FOR CHRISTIANS?

What binds all of the different writers, and their books, together in the Bible? The Bible itself provides us with an answer in extracts A and B. These verses only refer to the Old Testament, although they sum up what most Christians feel about the whole Bible.

A *"We know that what the Scripture says is true forever..."*

John 10.35

B *"For the word of God is living and active. Sharper than any two-edged sword, it penetrates even to the dividing of soul and spirit, joints and marrow; it judges the thoughts and attitudes of the heart."*

Hebrews 4.12

Christians believe that the Bible is special because it tells them what God demands of them. Some Christians believe that God delivered the Bible exactly as we have it today but most Christians believe that the writers of the books were 'inspired' by God, although the words they used were their own. This does not make the Bible any less important to them but it does mean that people must try to find the words of God behind the words of the Bible.

Reading the Bible is an important part of worship for many Christians.

WHAT USE DO CHRISTIANS MAKE OF THE BIBLE?

Christians use the Bible in two different ways:

- **In public worship.** All Christian acts of worship contain readings from the Bible. In an Anglican service, for example, there are usually three readings from the Bible – from the Old Testament, from the New Testament and from the letters in the New Testament. The priest or minister leading the service will also base his or her sermon on one of the passages.

- **In private worship.** Many Christians read a passage from the Bible each day as a way of encouraging their prayers. Some Christians use a passage from the Bible to help them to meditate.

OVER TO YOU ▶▶▶

1 Which word is used in extract A to refer to the writings of the Old Testament and what does it say about them?

2 What is described as being 'living and active' and what do you think this comment means?

TAKE TIME TO THINK

The Bible appears in the *Guinness Book of Records* as the most widely published book of all time. However, it has been said that: "The Bible is the most widely published book of all time yet it is the least read book in the world."

a) Do you think this is right?

b) If so, why do you think that the Bible is not read more widely?

There is more than one Bible reading in most church services.

THE AUTHORITY OF JESUS

You will find out

- What Christians believe about Jesus.

- What authority Jesus carries for Christians.

- How Christians believe that they can know Jesus today.

In the glossary

Bible

Cross

Gospel

Heaven

Holy Communion

Holy Spirit

Miracle

New Testament

Resurrection

Sermon

Sin

Trinity

CHRISTIANS AND JESUS

Almost all the information that we have about Jesus comes from the Gospels in the New Testament:

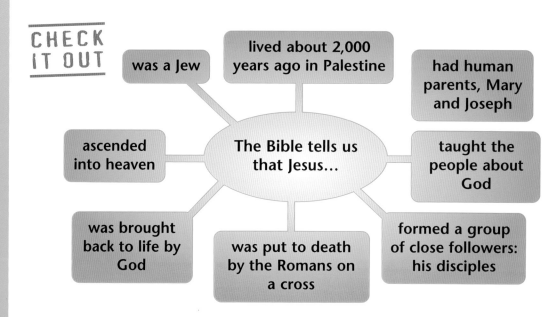

CHECK IT OUT

The Bible tells us that Jesus...

- lived about 2,000 years ago in Palestine
- was a Jew
- had human parents, Mary and Joseph
- taught the people about God
- formed a group of close followers: his disciples
- was put to death by the Romans on a cross
- was brought back to life by God
- ascended into heaven

Christians do, of course, believe more about Jesus than this. They also believe that:

- Jesus was divine – he was God's Son. He was part of the Christian Trinity of God the Father, God the Son and God the Holy Spirit.

- Jesus was human and died for the sins of the whole world. Jesus was sinless and so was able to die for others. Everyone who believes in Jesus will be saved.

- The Resurrection of Jesus from the dead brings eternal life to everyone who believes in him.

This is how a modern sculptor saw Jesus.

THE AUTHORITY OF JESUS

Christians believe that Jesus is both divine, God, and also the perfect human being. As a human being, he made known the will of God for all human beings by showing them how God expected them to live. By following his teachings, human beings can know that they are doing the will of God.

As God, Jesus carries unique authority for all Christians. The teachings of Jesus are found in the Gospels in the New Testament. Extract A shows a summary by one Gospel writer of the message of Jesus. The Gospels also record actions of Jesus which show his divine power – the miracles that he carried out over sickness, the powers of nature and death.

A *"The kingdom of God is near. Repent and believe the good news."*

Mark 4.17

KNOWING JESUS

Christians believe that Jesus is alive today. They find that reading the Bible and praying helps them to draw closer to God and to Jesus. Meeting with other Christians in worship and fellowship is also very important. The most important act of worship for most Christians is Holy Communion, during which eating bread and drinking wine is a powerful reminder to everyone of the death of Jesus. Hymns, prayers and sermons in church all encourage people to think about Jesus.

TAKE TIME TO THINK

Christians believe that Jesus is alive and with them each day. Yet he died 2,000 years ago. What do you think they mean when they say this?

Christians believe that Jesus overcame death for everyone by his own death and so is able to offer forgiveness to all.

OVER TO YOU ▶▶▶

1 Write a paragraph to describe what the Bible tells us about Jesus.
2 Write a paragraph to describe what Christians believe about Jesus.
3 Here are descriptions of three different kinds of miracles carried out by Jesus:
   a) Healing. Matthew 8.1-4
   b) Controlling the forces of nature. Matthew 8.23-27
   c) Overcoming death. Mark 5.21-43
   Write your own description of each of these miracles.

You will find out

- The meaning and importance of the words 'charisma' and 'vocation'.

- The meaning of Ordination.

- About the different leaders in the Roman Catholic, Anglican and Nonconformist Churches.

In the glossary

Archbishop

Bishop

Cardinal

Church of England

Diocese

Holy Spirit

Minister

Nonconformist Church

Ordination

Pope

Priest

Protestent Church

Quakers

Roman Catholic Church

Sacrament

Vicar

Vocation

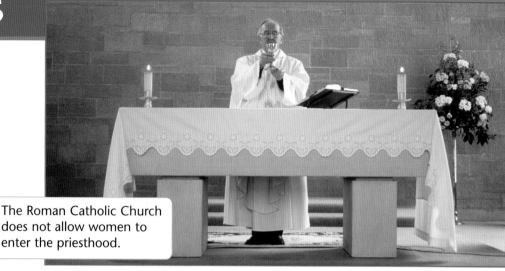

The Roman Catholic Church does not allow women to enter the priesthood.

CHARISMA AND VOCATION

Each religion has its own spiritual leaders. These are people who are highly respected for their wisdom and power to inspire others. They are also people who have two other qualities:

- They have charisma. This is the quality that makes a leader stand out from other people – whether they are politicians, sports or pop stars, or leaders in other fields. This is the power to inspire others to follow them and look up to them.

- They have a vocation. When someone feels called by God to follow a particular career path, they are said to have a 'calling' or **vocation**. The word is also applied to those people who enter careers such as nursing or teaching. It is certainly applied to those who become priests or ministers.

CHRISTIAN LEADERS

Men and women who wish to become spiritual leaders – whether as bishops, priests or ministers – are ordained. Ordination is one of the seven sacraments in the Roman Catholic Church. In this ceremony, a man is set aside to carry out a special work for God and given the power of the Holy Spirit to carry it out.

CHECK IT OUT

The Pope – the leader of the Roman Catholic Church.

Cardinals – the most important bishops in the Roman Catholic Church.

Ministers – men and women in the Nonconformist Churches who lead public worship.

Different Christian leaders

Bishops – senior priests in the Roman Catholic and Anglican churches.

Priests – those men and women who administer the sacraments in the Roman Catholic and Anglican churches.

In the Roman Catholic Church, the Pope is the supreme leader. On occasions he is believed to speak infallibly – which means that his teaching is to be believed by the whole Church. Underneath the Pope are many cardinals who choose the next Pope when one dies. The cardinals are chosen from those who are already bishops. A bishop has responsibility for all the churches in an area called a diocese.

The Church of England is the largest Protestant Church in Britain. The monarch is the head of the Church of England, taking the title of 'Defender of the Faith'. The Church is led on the ground by two **Archbishops** – the Archbishop of Canterbury [the senior] and the Archbishop of York [the junior]. Underneath the two Archbishops are many bishops who look after the churches in their **diocese**. Priests or vicars have responsibility for one or several churches. They are often helped by junior priests called curates.

There are many Nonconformist Churches, such as Baptist, Methodist and Pentecostal. They have their own ministers who look after individual churches. The Quakers are different from other Protestant denominations. They do not have priests or ministers. They believe in the 'priesthood of all believers', which means that anyone can be called upon to play a part in leading the congregation in their worship.

OVER TO **YOU** ▶▶▶

1 What do we mean when we use the words:
   a) Charisma?
   b) Vocation?

The Church of England voted to allow women into its priesthood in the early 1990s but women are still not allowed to become bishops.

DIFFERENT KINDS OF TRUTH

You will find out

- A very important question that Jesus was asked.

- What the different kinds of truth are.

- The places to which we all go to find out the truth.

In the glossary

Bible

Conscience

New Testament

Pope

Roman Catholic Church

The New Testament records a conversation between Jesus, on trial for his life, and Pontius Pilate, who was the Roman governor of the province. You can find the brief conversation that they had, during which Pilate asked Jesus a very important question, in extract A.

A "*Pilate asked him, 'Are you a king, then?' Jesus answered, 'You say that I am a king. I was born and came into the world for this one purpose, to speak about the truth. Whoever belongs to the truth listens to me.' 'And what is truth?' Pilate asked.*"

John 18.37-38

DIFFERENT KINDS OF TRUTH

Pilate did not wait to hear the answer of Jesus to the question, "What is truth?" It would have been interesting to hear what it was! We now know, however, that there are several different kinds of 'truth':

CHECK IT OUT

Intuitive truth – This is the truth that comes in the form of a 'gut feeling'. There may be good reasons for believing it – or not.

Historical truth – To find out the truth about the past, historians examine old documents or evidence from archaeology.

Religious truth – Christians believe that God has 'revealed' truths in the Bible and through Jesus. These truths could not be known unless God had revealed them.

Legal truth – A trial in court sets out to find the truth about a crime. A jury of twelve people is asked to decide what the truth is.

What is truth?

Scientific truth – To find out a scientific truth, an experiment must be conducted – and then repeated many times. The result must always be the same. This 'truth' can always be changed if someone proves something different by conducting another experiment.

Christians believe that religious truth is the most important form of truth. This is truth that people could never know unless God had chosen to reveal it to them. Some Christians would argue that, as God knows everything, so everything that we read in the Bible must be true. Any mistakes are because human beings, who are not perfect, have tried to pass that truth on to others.

The Bible is the best record that Christians have of God's will for them.

How do we find the truth?

All of us have ways of coming to terms with the world around us. It might be through:

- **Listening to others.** Our 'peer group' is the group of people who are of a similar age to ourselves. They are a major source of information but may not always be reliable.

- **Listening to our conscience.** We have already found out what our conscience is and how it works [unit 17]. Obviously our sense of right and wrong will tell us what to believe about ourselves and others. This 'inner voice' can show us where the truth is to be found.

- **Listening to our reason.** Human beings have been given the power to think. In many situations this allows them to decide between what is true and what is false. Many Christians believe that their power to think is a gift from God.

- **Listening to a higher authority.** Some people seek advice from people they respect when they want to know the truth. That person might be a spiritual or religious teacher. Many Roman Catholics, for example, look to the Pope for guidance. They may find God's authority in a holy book.

OVER TO YOU ▶▶▶

1 Do you feel more comfortable accepting certain kinds of truth rather than others? Try to explain why.

2 Are there any other kinds of 'truth' that you think should be added to this list? If so, what are they?

3 Working with your partner, try to produce examples of each of these different kinds of truth.

TAKE TIME TO THINK

Which of these four ways of finding the truth do you think is the most important in your life? Perhaps you turn to another source to find out the truth? If so, what is it?

MIRACLES

You will find out

- What people mean by the word 'miracle'.

- What the different kinds of miracles in the Bible are.

In the glossary

Bible

Miracle

New Testament

Old Testament

Paul

Resurrection

Synagogue

This stained-glass window shows Jesus raising the daughter of Jairus from the dead.

SAINT LVRE   Ch. VII V. 15

Miracles, or claims that a miracle has taken place, are very controversial. This is because a miracle seems to be a supernatural event that has broken the laws of nature. If an event has no natural explanation, the only explanation that many people can suggest is that God has been involved. If so, that would make it a miracle.

Here are two examples of events that people might claim to be miraculous:

- There are some cases of people praying to God for help and then being healed from diseases thought to be incurable.

- There are examples of people being rescued from collapsed buildings many days after an earthquake has taken place.

MIRACLES AND CHRISTIANITY

Christians believe that miracles are a religious experience. They are sure that God can perform miracles. If a miracle has really happened then it means that God has acted on Earth. Those who witnessed and experienced the miracle have been brought into direct contact with God as a result.

There are many miracles recorded in both the Old and New Testaments. In the New Testament, most, but not all, of them are linked with the life of Jesus. We are told, for example, that Jesus performed many healing miracles as well as miracles showing his authority over nature. He also brought more than one person back from the dead. You can find a description of one healing miracle in extract A.

A **"***While Jesus was still speaking, some men came from the house of Jairus, the synagogue ruler. 'Your daughter is dead,' they said. 'Why bother the teacher any more?' Ignoring what they said, Jesus told the synagogue ruler, 'Don't be afraid; just believe.' He took the child's father and mother and the disciples who were with him, and went in where the child was. He took her by the hand and said to her, 'Talitha Koum!' [which means 'Little girl, I say to you, get up'] Immediately the girl stood up and walked around.***"**

Mark 5.35-42

For Christians, however, one miracle is supremely important. This is the Resurrection of Jesus from the dead. Christians believe that God brought Jesus back to life three days after he had been crucified. This miracle is very important because it stands at the very centre of the Christian faith. Paul, in fact, wrote that if Jesus did not rise from the dead then the Christian religion is worthless.

MIRACLES OR CONJURING TRICKS?

In 2006, an interesting series of programmes was shown on Channel 4 as two American illusionists recreated miracles from both the Old and New Testaments. Some people believe that the miracles in the Bible were little more than conjuring tricks carried out on people who were easily taken in.

Certainly people who do not believe in God do not believe that miracles are possible. They say that there must be some other explanation. Religious people, however, claim that their faith in God is strengthened by such extraordinary events.

OVER TO YOU ▶▶▶

1 Look at the two examples on the opposite page. If you had found yourself in either situation, would you call it a 'miracle'? Try to explain your answer.

2 Have you heard or read about any incident which you think might be called a 'miracle'? What do other people in your class think about it?

3 Imagine that you are one of the observers of the miracle which is recorded in extract A. You could be one of the disciples or the parents of the little girl. Write up a description of the event as you see it and include an illustration or two.

TAKE TIME TO THINK

Do you believe that miracles happen? Give two reasons for your belief – whatever it is. Is there one event which you think is so extraordinary that it persuades you that miracles could happen?

RELIGION AND SCIENCE – FRIENDS OR ENEMIES?

You will find out

- About the very important part played by science in modern life.

- Whether science and religion are enemies.

- Which two scientific theories have most disturbed religion in the past.

In the glossary

Bible

Evolution

Priest

For centuries people have tried to make sense of the universe beyond them, the world in which they live and their own bodies. To do this they have used both religion and science. Since the 18th century, however, science has become increasingly important in our attempt to gain real understanding. People have come to understand that science is only possible if the whole of life has a sense of order and design about it. For some people, religion and science go hand in hand in this quest, although many people doubt whether religion has a lot to offer. Here is a typical comment from the past:

A *"I was merely thinking God's thoughts after him."*

Johannes Kepler [1571-1630], German astronomer

ARE RELIGION AND SCIENCE FRIENDS OR ENEMIES?

To hear some people talk, you would think that religion and science were at each other's throats. It is a fact, however, that you will often hear religious people and scientists asking the same questions – such as:

- How did the universe begin?

- How did human life begin?

- Where does sickness and disease come from?

Christians who base their answers to these questions on the Bible will come up with very different answers to those given to us by science. Religion does, though, ask some very awkward questions of science:

- Is it right to use animals in scientific experiments?

- Is it right to transplant organs from one human being to another?

- Should human beings have the right to end their life early if they are suffering from a terminal [fatal] illness?

- Is stem cell technology a good thing?

All of these things are scientifically possible. Religion asks whether it is right that they take place. Certainly, over the centuries, many Christians have found it very difficult to accept certain scientific discoveries and theories. Two, in particular, have caused severe difficulties in the past:

- The discovery by the Christian priest and astronomer Nicolaus Copernicus [1473-1543] that the Earth revolves around the sun and not the other way round. Christians saw this as a huge loss of dignity for God's greatest creation – human beings.

- The theory of **evolution** put forward by Charles Darwin [1809-82] which suggested that human beings were superior animals who had finally arrived on Earth after millions of years of change and development. Christians saw this as an attack on God the Creator.

Charles Darwin, whose theory of evolution in the 19th century caused many Christians to believe that their faith was in direct conflict with science.

OVER TO **YOU** ▶▶▶

1   Look at extract A. Do you think that a scientist today might feel the same as Kepler – or not?

2   Write down four things that you find really surprising about the universe, the world or yourselves. Do you think that religion or science can help you to find out more about them? Give a reason for each of your answers.

3   Work on this one with your partner. Write down five difficult or awkward questions that a Christian might ask of a scientist.

TAKE TIME TO THINK

Eventually the scientist will be able to answer most, if not all, questions about the universe, the world in which we live and human beings. Do you think that this will make religion, and a belief in God, unnecessary?

SCIENCE AND THE CREATION OF LIFE

You will find out

- About genetic engineering – its value and dangers.

- About fertility treatment – its value and dangers.

- About cloning – its value and dangers.

In the glossary

Cloning

Embryo

Genetic engineering

In unit 24, we saw how religion asks awkward questions of new scientific discoveries and 'advances'. We also discovered that, just because something is scientifically possible, does not necessarily mean that it is the good or the right thing to do. This is particularly true in three very important areas of scientific work:

GENETIC ENGINEERING

Genetic engineering is using our knowledge about the genetic makeup of every human being to correct defective genes and so eliminate such diseases as Multiple Sclerosis and Huntingdon's Disease. It is already scientifically possible for parents to choose the sex of their child before it is conceived using genetic engineering.

A great debate is also taking place about whether we should grow genetically modified food. We can now make our food resistant to disease or extremes of the weather. We can offer other countries which suffer from widespread hunger much more plentiful and reliable food supplies. Some people think this is the only effective answer to hunger in the world. Others, though, are far less sure as the questions asked below make clear:

> Where do we stop with genetic engineering for human beings? Is the next stop 'designer babies'?

> Should we try to eradicate all disability and illness?

> What happens if genetically modified plants cross-pollinate and so everyone's food is affected?

> Do we know enough about genetically modified food to be sure that the health of people is not at risk? Is it completely reliable? Does it have any long-term effects?

CLONING

Recently, scientists have found a way of **cloning** plants and animals. They do this by taking the DNA from one animal or plant and transferring it to another of the same species. Soon it might be possible to do this with a human being, so making a new person. In 1997, scientists in Scotland announced that they had cloned a sheep called 'Dolly'. She was made from the cells of two different sheep and no ram was involved. In Britain, it is legal to create replacement tissue and organs and this will offer future cures for many diseases.

FERTILITY TREATMENT

10% of all couples have difficulty conceiving a baby. People in this group would not become parents unless they were given some kind of medical help. There are different ways of doing this:

- **In vitro fertilisation.** 'In vitro' means 'in a glass' and people often call this having a 'test-tube baby'. The technique was developed to help women who have a blockage in their fallopian tubes. As a result, their eggs could not reach their uterus to be fertilised by a male sperm. The woman's eggs are collected, removed from her body, fertilised by her partner's sperm and replaced in her body. Both the woman's eggs and her partner's sperm are used.

- **Artificial insemination by donor [AID].** If the man is infertile then sperm from an anonymous donor are placed in the woman's body. The woman has a baby, although its father is not her partner/ husband.

- **Artificial insemination by the partner/husband [AIH].** The husband's sperm are collected and placed in the woman's body. The woman becomes pregnant by her husband/partner.

- **Surrogacy.** This happens when a woman agrees to have a baby for someone else who cannot have one.

In 1990, some guidelines for fertility treatment became law. These stated that infertility is a good reason for having IVF treatment. Any research performed on **embryos** produced by this treatment must be carried out within 14 days.

TAKE TIME TO THINK

Do you think that cloning should be used to change what children might look like – or even how they behave?

OVER TO **YOU** ▶▶▶

1 Explain what is meant by:
   a) AIH
   b) AID
   c) Surrogacy

This is Dolly the Sheep. Does cloning like this throw up many dangers for the future? Many people think so.

THE CHRISTIAN RESPONSE

You will find out

- Christian beliefs and the scientific ability to create life.

- The Christian belief that all life is sacred and holy.

- The Christian belief that human beings are created in the image of God.

In the glossary

Abortion

Adultery

Cloning

Embryo

Genetic Engineering

Miracle

Soul

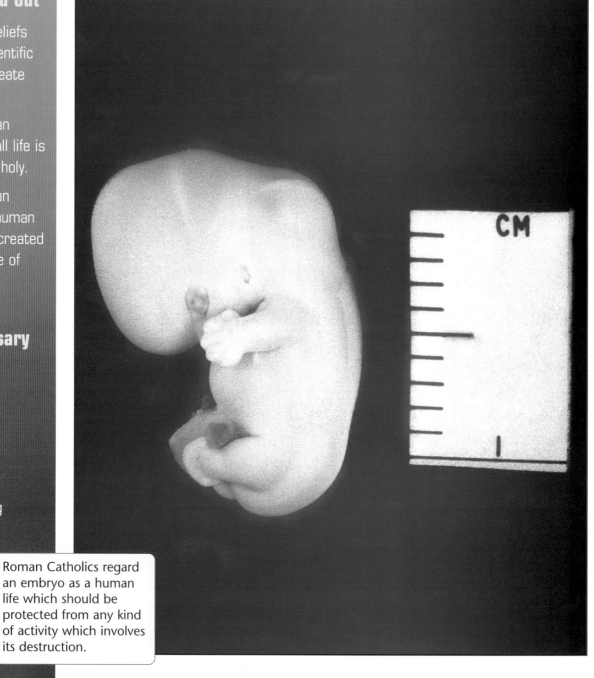

Roman Catholics regard an embryo as a human life which should be protected from any kind of activity which involves its destruction.

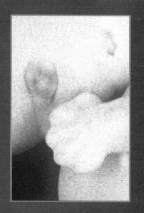

In unit 25, we looked at different ways that scientists could either create or change human life. Many Christians have seen this as a direct challenge to their religious faith. What beliefs do Christians hold which seem to be directly challenged by these developments?

BELIEF 1: THAT ALL LIFE IS HOLY

Many Christians, especially Roman Catholics, see genetic engineering as a direct challenge to their belief that all life is given by God – and is holy. They are worried about embryos which are created and then discarded as part of the treatment. This they see as the same thing as **abortion**. They see artificial insemination by donor [AID] as a form of **adultery**.

BELIEF 2: THAT ALL LIFE COMES FROM GOD

Many Christians return to the story of creation in the book of Genesis [chapters 1-3], where God's creation of all forms of life is described as 'perfect'. They believe that such things as genetic engineering and cloning are an attempt to improve on God's perfect creation. The same applies to human attempts to change or improve plants and other natural parts of creation.

It is argued that scientists are attempting to 'play God'. By interfering with nature, scientists are playing a very dangerous game. No-one knows what the outcome of this interference will be.

BELIEF 3: THAT HUMAN BEINGS ARE SPIRITUAL CREATURES

We saw in unit 17 the Christian belief that all human beings have souls. Some Christians believe that cloning is very dangerous because it opens the door to the cloning of human beings – although every authority is totally opposed to this. Some Christians ask how science could implant a soul in a cloned human being.

BELIEF 4: THAT HUMAN BEINGS ARE MADE IN GOD'S IMAGE

This is a very important statement found in the story of creation – that human beings are created in God's image. It is this that makes them different, and superior, to any of the animals. Is this image destroyed if scientists begin to tinker with the human race? Christians have always maintained that birth is a miracle. As much as we know about it and understand it, there is always something miraculous about it – ask any parent and they will tell you! Does the same feeling remain after a baby is conceived by IVF? Do people created artificially still bear the image of God?

BELIEF 5: THAT ALL HUMAN BEINGS ARE INDIVIDUALS

Genetic engineering and cloning make it possible to remove defects before a baby is born. Many people, Christians among them, would argue that this can only be a good thing. Yet the presence of physically handicapped people in the world teaches people to be more caring and compassionate in the way that they treat others.

There are great dangers in parents being able to create the children that they want. The wide variety now present in the human family would begin to disappear. Many Christians view this drift towards the creation of 'designer babies' with horror.

OVER TO YOU ▶▶▶

1 Explain what is meant by:
   a) Abortion
   b) Adultery

2 Discuss this statement with other members of your class. "God has created the world and human beings the way they are. We should accept this and not try to change things."

3 If we are drifting towards the creation of 'designer babies', do you think that would be a good or a bad thing? What would you welcome? What would you dread?

TAKE TIME TO THINK

What do you think it means when people say that man is made in God's image? If you believed this, do you think it would affect the way that you lived your life? How?

VIVISECTION

You will find out

- What is meant by 'vivisection'.

- The arguments for and against vivisection.

- The attitudes of Christians towards vivisection.

In the glossary

Bible

Steward

Vivisection

Carrying out scientific experiments on animals [called **vivisection**] is a highly controversial scientific activity. In the early years of the 21st century, a series of protests, often very violent, were carried out against Huntingdon Life Sciences in Cambridge because it performed experiments on live animals for scientific research.

There are two clear arguments for and against vivisection:

- There can be no doubt that, in the past, such experiments have been important – leading to vaccines against diphtheria, polio and rubella, among other diseases. Although there are alternatives to vivisection, it is still necessary in the fight against disease.

- In the past, animals have been used to test for trivial reasons – such as new and better toiletries, like deodorants. These tests could have been carried out using computer simulation and cell-culture. This has led many people to wonder if animals are now unnecessary for scientific experiments. Little of this kind of experimentation now goes on. Today most companies do not use animals to test their products. The Body Shop, a highly successful company, stopped using animals to improve its products in 1990 and many other companies soon followed suit.

The whole issue of whether animals should be used in scientific and medical experiments arouses very strong feelings – on both sides.

Not surprisingly, the population is divided over vivisection. According to surveys, the majority seem to believe that it is justified if it leads us to a better understanding of, and cure for, diseases which still kill thousands of people. The minority, however, argue that experiments on animals are unnecessary in the modern world since better alternatives are available.

CHRISTIANS AND VIVISECTION

As you can see from extract A, the Bible seems to support the argument that animals have few, if any, rights. The story of creation appears to give human beings complete power over them and the freedom to use animals for their own ends.

A *"They [human beings] will have power over the fish, the birds, and all animals, domestic and wild, large and small."*

Genesis 1.26

The attitude simply was that God had created all of the animals for man's benefit. Most Christians have gone along with this in the past. Now, however, attitudes have changed and Christians are much more sensitive to the humane treatment of animals. In particular, the Christian Churches teach that:

- Experiments carried out on animals for essential medical research are necessary and acceptable.

- The value of animal life is less than that of human life. Any experiments, however, should always be carried out humanely and without causing any unnecessary pain.

- Trivial experiments, such as the testing of cosmetics, should never be performed on animals.

- Human beings do not have dominion and power over animals. They are called by God to be stewards or guardians over the whole of the natural world, including the animal kingdom.

- The book of Genesis records how the first human beings were told by God to name all the animals. This was an ancient way of saying that the animals were lower than human beings.

OVER TO **YOU** ▶▶▶

1 Do you think that animals have 'rights' as well as human beings? If so, what do you think some of those rights are?

2 Which side of this argument do you come down on? You must be able to produce two arguments to support your point of view.

TAKE TIME TO THINK

Do you think that, if it could be proved that animal experiments would lead to cures for some of the world's worst diseases, that most people would support them?

ORGAN TRANSPLANTATION

You will find out

- About organ transplantation and the organs that can be transplanted.

- The important questions raised by transplantation, whether the donor is alive or dead.

- What xenotransplantation is and the questions it raises.

- The Christian and Humanist attitudes to organ transplants.

In the glossary

Humanist

Xenotransplantation

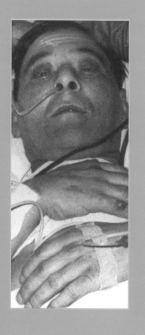

The first organ transplantation took place as long ago as 1905, when a cornea was replaced in an eye. In the last 25 years, it has become possible to replace at least 25 different organs and tissues – including bone and cartilage tissues, kidney, pancreas, heart, lung and liver. These operations were revolutionary when they were first introduced but they are almost commonplace now. They are giving thousands of people a new lease of life.

Organ transplantation brings some hotly debated issues to the surface. Among these, the scarcity of available organs making organ transplantation a bit of a lottery and the use of animal organs and tissues when human organs are not available [**xenotransplantation**].

QUESTIONS RAISED BY ORGAN TRANSPLANTATION

The donors of organs for transplantation fall into two groups:

- Transplants in which the donor is still living. This might be the donation of bone marrow or of a kidney. The important thing is that there must be a perfect match between the donor and the recipient, which means that the donor is usually a relative. People can live a normal life with only one kidney. In the UK it is illegal for someone to be paid to donate an organ, although it sometimes happens in other countries. The important thing is that, if the donor is still alive, they can give consent for the organ to be taken.

- Transplants in which the donor is dead. This might take place after the donor has died in a car accident or in some other way. Many people carry donor cards or go on a computerised register giving permission for their organs to be used if they die suddenly or unexpectedly. The major problem is that the organ must be removed very soon after death and close relatives sometimes find this very distressing. This is much easier if a donor card is being carried or the person's name is on the NHS Organ Donor Register.

XENOTRANSPLANTATION

We have already said that there is a great shortage of suitable organs for transplantation – whether hearts, kidneys or other parts of the body. It is becoming increasingly possible for animal organs to be used to make up for this shortage. This does, however, raise several important questions:

- There is a high risk of animal organs being rejected by the recipient's body. Should that risk be taken?
- Should animals be specially bred for this purpose?
- Transplants are very expensive. Should money be spent in this way?
- How would people feel about having animal organs in their own body?
- Eventually we might be able to replace almost any organ that wears out or becomes diseased. Would that be a good thing?

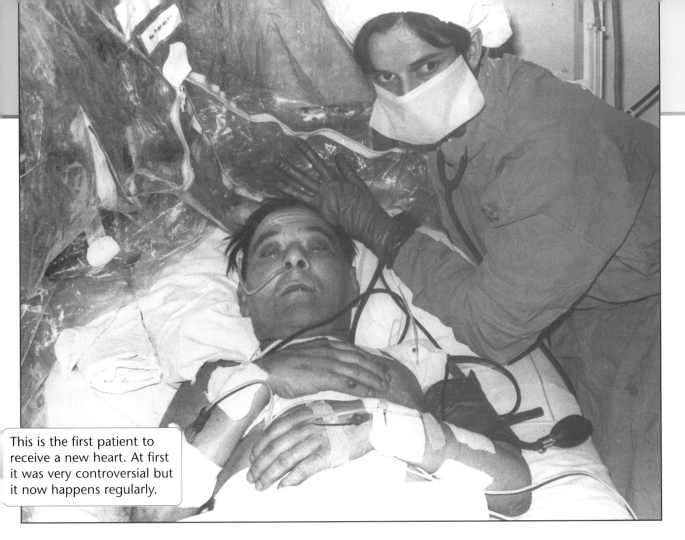

This is the first patient to receive a new heart. At first it was very controversial but it now happens regularly.

CHRISTIANS, HUMANISTS AND ORGAN TRANSPLANTATION

Most Christians follow the teaching of Jesus [A] and believe that it is a very good thing to be able to donate one of their own organs to give someone else life. Few Christians would feel unhappy if someone else, alive or dead, passed one of their organs on to them.

A *"The greatest love a person can have for his friends is to give his life for them."*

John 15.13

Humanists do not believe in an after-life and so they think that it is this life that matters. They argue that being willing to donate organs for others is the best way of making sure that others have a good quality of life. Although it is a good thing to offer one's organs, it must remain a person's personal choice or that of their closest relatives.

TAKE TIME TO THINK

Because not enough people offer their organs when they die, it is suggested that there should be a major change. Instead of opting into the scheme it should be assumed that everyone is willing to donate their organs unless they opt out. What do you think of this suggestion? Would you be happy with it?

OVER TO **YOU** ▶▶▶

1 Would you be prepared to carry a donor card so that your organs could be used to help someone else if you suddenly died?

2 Imagine that your brother or sister was to suffer from kidney failure and your kidney was the only perfect match. Would you be willing to donate one of your kidneys to them? Would you feel the same way if the person in need was a stranger?

3 There are many important questions asked above. Discuss some of them with your partner.

You will find out

- What the conscience is.

- What humanists believe about the conscience.

- How Christians believe that their conscience is 'the voice of God'.

- How many Christians believe in Satan as the source of all evil.

In the glossary

Bible

Conscience

Free Will

Humanist

Satan

Sin

Scientists tell us that human beings are advanced animals and this is biologically correct. There are, however, many important ways in which human beings and animals are different. One of the most important differences is that human beings know the difference between right and wrong. You will not find a dog worrying about whether he was right to have a go at the postman or not!

This raises, then, a very important question. How can human beings know what is the right thing to do? As we saw in unit 17, there is something, called the conscience, deep inside all of us which gives us a clear sense of what is right and wrong. From an early age, people around us – especially our friends and parents – also influence the way we think and behave.

HUMANISTS, CHRISTIANS AND THE CONSCIENCE

As we have seen, humanists do not believe in God but they do believe that everyone has a conscience. They believe that their conscience is a warning mechanism which informs them of the consequences of each action. If we ignore it, as we are perfectly able to do, and go against it then it makes us feel uneasy. This is why people sometimes speak of their conscience 'pricking' them. Many people remember this when they are next faced with a similar decision and, if they are sensible, they make sure that they do not make the same mistake again.

Where, though, does the conscience come from if it is not from God? The humanist answer is that it is part of everyone's character and that it is developed as they grow up through their contacts with other people – especially their parents.

The Christian religion teaches that God has given free will to all human beings. This simply means that they are free to live their lives as they choose. In particular, human beings are able to choose whether to obey God or not and whether to do the right or the wrong thing. Christians believe that evil occurs, in particular, when men and women choose to disobey God.

Many Christians believe the story in the book of Genesis which describes how the first man and woman, Adam and Eve, chose to disobey God and introduced sin into the world [Genesis chapter 3]. Many also believe that there is a supernatural force, **Satan**, who tempts human beings to commit sinful actions. Satan appears in the Bible as the great enemy of God – a fallen angel who rebelled against God's authority.

Humanists do not, of course, believe in Satan. They believe that everyone should treat other people as they would like to be treated themselves. Evil arises when other people fail to do this and treat others selfishly and thoughtlessly.

TAKE TIME TO THINK

Someone has said that it isn't always easy to do what is right but it is always right to do what is right. Do you agree with them?

1 Discuss with your partner how you have been influenced by your friends and parents in knowing the difference between right and wrong. List five things that you have learned from your friends and five things from your parents.

2 a) Do you have a conscience?
   b) How do you know?
   c) Where do you think it comes from?
   d) How does your conscience communicate with you?

3 A recent opinion poll suggested that 7 out of every 10 people believe in a personal Devil. Do you share this opinion? Explain your answer, whatever it is.

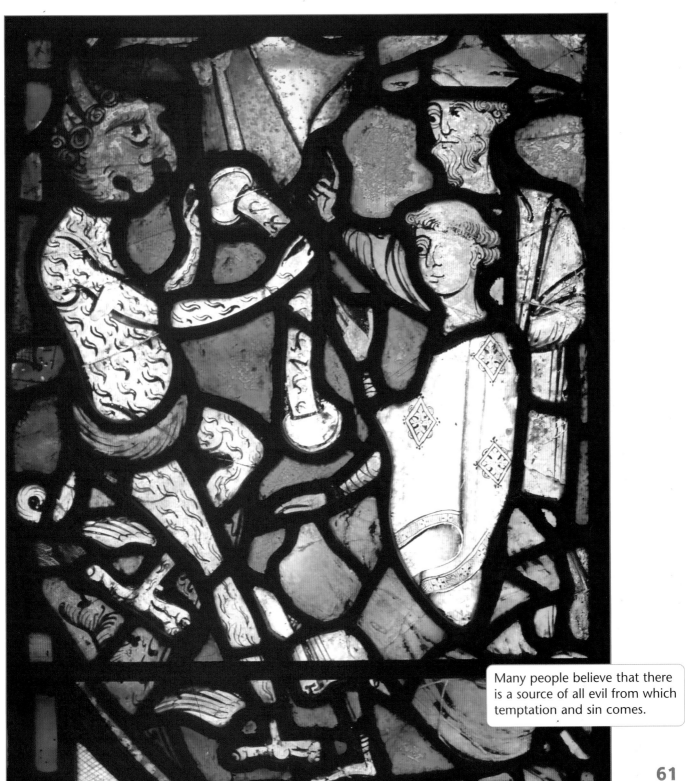

Many people believe that there is a source of all evil from which temptation and sin comes.

You will find out

- Some of the ways that Christians are helped in their everyday lives.

- The value the Ten Commandments have for Christians today.

- The help that Christians receive from the teachings of Jesus.

In the glossary

Adultery

Bible

Church

New Testament

Sabbath Day

Ten Commandments

Many people are guided in their daily decision-making by their religious faith. This is certainly true for Christians and the opinions given by the two Christians below are typical:

> When I became a Christian five years ago, I knew nothing about the Bible or its teachings. Since then I have read a passage from the Bible each day. I find that this helps me to discover what God wants me to do and I try to put those teachings into practice each day.

[Andrew, 31, lives in the East End of London]

> I have been a Christian for as long as I can remember. I go to church as often as I can and find that meeting with other Christians gives me a lot of help in my daily life. We also meet most weeks to talk about any problems that we have and this helps me a lot.

[Nina, 19, is a student in Birmingham]

As these two comments make clear, most Christians receive a lot of help from other believers – and also from the Bible. Many Christians try to live their lives by the principles that are found in the Ten Commandments. You can find a shortened version of these old laws in extract A.

A **"YOU SHALL HAVE NO OTHER GODS BEFORE ME. DO NOT CREATE IMAGES OF ANYTHING TO WORSHIP THEM. DO NOT USE MY HOLY NAME FOR YOUR OWN PURPOSES. KEEP THE SABBATH DAY AS A HOLY DAY. SHOW YOUR FATHER AND MOTHER ALL THE RESPECT THEY DESERVE. DO NOT KILL ANYONE. DO NOT COMMIT ADULTERY WITH ANYONE. DO NOT STEAL. DO NOT ACCUSE ANYONE FALSELY. DO NOT DESIRE TO POSSESS SOMEONE ELSE'S HOUSE – OR ANYTHING ELSE THAT BELONGS TO HIM."**

Exodus 20.3-17

To help one another in living their Christian lives, groups of young Christians often meet together to talk.

Christians find that these are very helpful in providing them with a 'route-map' to help them to find their way through life. No-one can pretend that life in the time of Jesus was the same as life is today. As you will find out later, there are many problems today that Christians in the lifetime of Jesus did not have to face.

Here are two sayings of Jesus that Christians find very helpful to follow:

B *"Love the Lord your God with all your heart and with all your soul and with all your mind and with all your strength."*

Mark 12.30

C *"Love your neighbour as yourself."*

Mark 12.31

OVER TO **YOU** ▶▶▶

1 Talk about the Ten Commandments with other members of your class.

   a) Which of the Ten Commandments do you think is the most difficult to keep? Give one reason for your answer.

   b) Which of the Ten Commandments do you think is most often broken today? Try to explain why.

2 A website recently invited people to write one new commandment to bring the old Ten Commandments up to date. Which new commandments would you want to add to the list and which would you omit altogether?

3 Think of two ways in which the society in which you live could be improved as a place to live. Do you think that this could happen – or is it just a dream?

WHAT ARE HUMAN RIGHTS?

You will find out

- The United Nations Declaration on Human Rights.

- The work of Amnesty International.

- The parable of the Good Samaritan.

In the glossary

Archbishop

Bible

Conscience

Parable

The work of Amnesty International is admired throughout the world for the work it does to support those whose human rights are being denied.

A very important event took place on 10th December 1948. The world was recovering from the atrocities that had taken place during World War Two and 51 countries came together to draw up a list of those freedoms that should be enjoyed by every human being. You can find some of them in extract A.

A "1. All human beings are born equal irrespective of their sex, race, colour, religion or age.
2. Each person should enjoy personal liberty and freedom.
3. No-one should be a slave.
4. No-one should be tortured.
5. Everyone should be equal in the eyes of the law.
6. Everyone should have freedom of movement.
7. All men and women should be free to marry the partner of their choice.
8. Everyone should have the right to own their own property.
9. Everyone should have freedom of opinion, conscience and thought.
10. Everyone has the right to be in paid employment."

The remainder of the 20th century saw a constant struggle to extend these rights to every human being. As the 21st century began, they remained but a distant dream for millions of people. This is a matter of deep concern to Christians who believe that God has created all people equal. In extract B, you can find some quotations from the Bible which make this clear:

B   *"So God created man [and woman] in his own image."*

Genesis 1.27

"From one man he made every nation of men, that they should inhabit the whole earth, and he determined the times set for them and the exact places where they should live."

Acts 17.36

"There is neither Jew nor Greek, slave nor free, male nor female, for you are all one in Christ Jesus."

Galatians 3.28

OVER TO **YOU** ▶▶▶

1   Look carefully at the ten freedoms in extract A. Give some examples from modern life of these freedoms being threatened – or being denied altogether.

2   Why do you think that governments so often deny human rights to their citizens? What could they be frightened of?

3   You can read the parable of the Good Samaritan for yourself in Luke 10.25-37. Combine this account with the extracts from the Bible in B and write down three reasons why Christians should be concerned by the mistreatment of other human beings.

4   This quote comes from a speech of Archbishop Desmond Tutu: "Christian worship can never let us be indifferent to the needs of others, to the cries of the hungry, of the naked, and the homeless, of the sick and of the prisoner, of the oppressed and disadvantaged." Write a paragraph explaining why Christians like Archbishop Tutu need to be strongly in favour of human rights.

AMNESTY INTERNATIONAL

Amnesty International was formed in 1961, to bring abuses of human rights around the world out into the open. It works to:

- Secure the abolition of the Death Penalty worldwide. It is still retained in over 70 countries.
- Bring about the abolition of the use of torture everywhere to obtain information from prisoners.
- Secure a fair and speedy trial for all those arrested.
- Secure the release of 'prisoners of conscience' from prison.

A 'prisoner of conscience' is someone who has been arrested and imprisoned because of sincerely held religious or political beliefs – and not for committing a criminal act.

C   *"Amnesty International is engaged in what is often a life or death struggle to defend human rights in many countries all over the world... Only by becoming a mass movement for human rights can we hope to play our full part in ending the international hypocrisy which surrounds the plight of so many in the world... Amnesty's sole reason for existence is to campaign against torture and execution and for the release of men and women imprisoned for their beliefs, colour, ethnic origin, language and religion..."*

Amnesty International Leaflet

Many Christians support the work of Amnesty International. They have been inspired by the parable of the Good Samaritan told by Jesus. In this story it is clear that it is the person who acts practically to help others who does the will of God.

TAKING RESPONSIBILITY FOR OTHER

You will find out

- About Christian responsibility for helping those who are strangers.

- About Christian responsibility for those in need.

In the glossary

Bible

Gospel

Heaven

New Testament

Salvation Army

HELPING THOSE WHO ARE STRANGERS

In unit 31, we looked at the work of Amnesty International. Although not a Christian organisation, Amnesty International provides us with a good example of the need for all human beings to take responsibility for the welfare of total strangers in need. Jesus had something important to say about this in extract A:

> A *"I was hungry and you gave me something to eat, I was thirsty and you gave me something to drink, I was a stranger and you invited me in, I needed clothes and you clothed me, was sick and you looked after me, I was in prison and you came to visit me... I tell you the truth, whatever you did for one of the least of these my brothers you did for me."*
>
> Matthew 25.35,40

Christians always look to Jesus for inspiration. They find that the four Gospels are full of examples of Jesus helping people who were complete strangers. In fact, it made no difference whether he knew them or not. All that mattered was that they were human beings and that Jesus could meet their need. If someone who was sick approached Jesus, for example, he healed them.

Christians feel the need to follow the example of Jesus. Here are some ways in which they try to do this:

- Some spend time on the streets bringing food, clothing and help to those who are homeless. The London City Mission has done this, for example, for over a century on the streets of London.

- The Salvation Army offers a tracing service to people who have lost contact with relatives in the UK and overseas.

- Many Christians are involved with different organisations offering specialised help to people with drug and alcohol-related problems.

HELPING THOSE IN NEED

To make people sit up and take notice, Jesus sometimes said things that he did not necessarily expect them to take literally. You can find one example of this in extract B:

> B *"...Go, sell everything you have and give to the poor, and you will have treasure in heaven."*
>
> Mark 14.21

Some Christians, however, have taken Jesus at his word. Perhaps the outstanding example in recent years has been that of Mother Teresa, who spent many years working among the destitute of Calcutta simply because she felt that this was what God wanted her to do.

The New Testament suggests that a person's religious beliefs must be married to action and practical help if that belief is to mean anything. You can see this by looking at extract C.

C "*What good is it, my brothers, if a man claims to have faith but has no deeds? Can such faith save him? Suppose a brother or sister is without clothes and daily food. If one of you says to him, 'Go, I wish you well; keep warm and well fed,' but does nothing about his physical needs, what good is it?*"

James 2.14-16

GIVING TO CHARITY

Night after night, images of suffering and poverty are beamed into our homes from many different parts of the world. In 2006, the most powerful images have come from the Middle East and particularly Lebanon. This has led to thousands of people, both religious and non-religious, wanting to help.

Giving to one of the many charities which exist to help those in need is, perhaps, the best place to start. All charities need those who will give regularly even if only a small amount. Some of the charities have flag-days when house-to-house collections are made and help is always needed for these. For these people, this is a small way of helping the world to move to a fairer way of living in which all people can share.

Jesus suggested that even the simplest actions to help those in need were pleasing to God.

OVER TO **YOU** ▶▶▶

1 Put the quotation that you find in extract A into your own words.

2 Draw six illustrations to show those people in need that Jesus suggested his followers should set out to help.

3 There are three quotations from the Bible in this unit. Rewrite each of them in your own words and explain what they have to say about the Christian way of life.

4 Compose a poem of eight lines to express your response to a scene of poverty or despair that you have recently seen on your television screen.

WHAT ARE 'ULTIMATE QUESTIONS'?

You will find out

- What an 'ultimate question' is.
- Examples of the 'ultimate questions' that people ask.

In the earlier parts of this book, we have looked at some of the beliefs that Christians hold and the reasons why they hold them. We have also looked at the influence that these beliefs have on the people who hold them. For many people, the beliefs that they hold go a long way to helping them to make sense of the world in which they live.

In particular, Christians feel that their beliefs provide them with some answers to the biggest questions about life – the questions that we all ask at some time or another. These are the most difficult questions of all to answer. This is why they are called 'ultimate questions', because they confront us with issues to do with the meaning of life and death.

You will explore some of these 'ultimate questions' in this unit. As you will see in the diagram, they go to the very heart of who we are and why we are here.

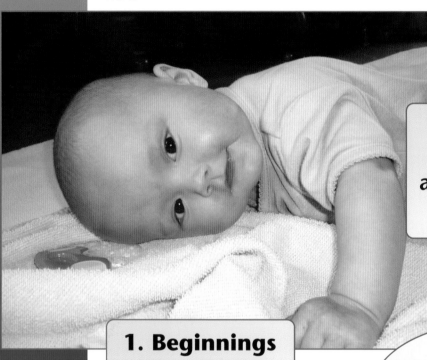

2. Belief
Does God exist and, if so, what is he like?

1. Beginnings
How did life begin and who made us?

What are the ultimate questions?

4. The future
What happens to me when I die?

OVER TO **YOU** ▶▶▶

1 Look carefully at the questions in the diagram.

　a) Do you think that these questions are particularly important? If so, try to explain why they really matter.

　b) Do you have any ideas about the answers to two of these questions?

　c) Does the rest of your class agree with your answers to these questions – or not?

2 Keep in the back of your mind what you already know about other religions. How do you think that a religious person might answer two of these questions?

3 Work with your partner to come up with an 'ultimate question' that has not been asked in the diagram. Remember – an 'ultimate question' has to do with life and its meaning or death and what happens beyond the grave.

TAKE TIME TO THINK

Take two of the questions that you see in the diagram. Why do you think that they might particularly interest:

a) A doctor?

b) A vicar?

c) A scientist?

3. Life
Why is there so much suffering?

You will find out

- What the developed world is.

- What the developing world is.

- The differences between the developed and the developing worlds.

In the glossary

Developed World

Developing World

HIV

Today we live in a divided world – one that is split between the wealthy people [known as the **developed world**] and the poor people [known as the **developing world**]. Extract A, taken from the United Nations Declaration of Human Rights, explains what every person wants from life:

> **A** *"...freedom from fear and want has been proclaimed as the highest aspiration of the common people..."*
>
> United Nations Declaration of Human Rights

THE DEVELOPED WORLD

The developed world consists of those countries that have a very high standard of living and includes:

- North America
- Western Europe
- Australasia

25% of the world's population [about 1,700 million people] live in the developed world. These countries, however, use 80% of all the world's resources, such as food and energy.

THE DEVELOPING WORLD

This part of the world includes those countries which have a very low standard of living. The developing world includes most of:

- South America
- India
- Africa

These countries have 75% of the world's population [about 5,400 million people] and yet live off just 20% of the world's resources.

Scenes like this from the developing countries emphasise that poverty is getting worse – not better.

AN UNEQUAL WORLD – FACTS AND FIGURES

Developing countries have:

- **a very high level of illiteracy** [the inability to read and write]. 1 in every 5 people in the developing world is illiterate. Schools are few and far between and those that do exist have scarce resources – with a lack of teachers. There is a direct link between illiteracy and poverty. It is almost impossible for illiterate people [about 1,000 million in the world] to lift themselves out of poverty.

- **a high level of malnutrition.** About 25% of the world's population is trying to exist on the equivalent of 50p a day! Millions of people do not have enough food to eat or are eating food with little nutritional value. While the world produces enough food for each person to have 3,000 calories a day, 600 million people live daily on less than 1,800 calories.

- **a lack of clean drinking water.** Millions walk long distances each day to find water – and then have to carry it back home again! It's a fact that:

  - 25 million people die each year from water-borne diseases.
  - 2.4 billion [30% of the world's population] do not have adequate sanitation.
  - 2 billion do not have access to clean drinking water.

  The effect of all this on the health of millions of people in developing countries is devastating.

- **many health problems brought about by poor health services.** It's a fact that:

  - Over 15 million children a year die from malnutrition. This is the equivalent of 25% of the population of the United Kingdom.
  - Developing countries have few doctors, nurses, hospitals or clinics.
  - **HIV**/AIDS is a growing problem, with more than 30 million worldwide now infected. You can find out more about this in unit 37.
  - Even where hospitals and clinics do exist, there is a great shortage of drugs.

OVER TO **YOU** ▶▶▶

1. Explain what is meant by:
   a) A 'developed country'.
   b) A 'developing country'.

2. Do you live in a developed or a developing country? How can you tell?

3. You have been asked to give a talk to your class on the differences between rich and poor countries in the world. Write down ten points that you would make so that your speech was as powerful as possible.

AS A RESULT

Because of these very poor facilities, many countries have a very low life expectancy. In some countries, people cannot expect to get far beyond their 40th birthday. This compares with a life expectancy of 75 years for men and 80 years for women in the UK.

As you can see, we live in a very unequal and unfair world. In a truly fair world, everyone would have the same opportunities and rights as everyone else. This is far from the case. In many instances, this is prevented by corruption and dishonesty in the poor countries. It is also caused by the trade practices of the rich countries, which give them an unfair advantage.

You will find out

- The teachings of the New Testament on wealth and poverty.

- What your own response is to the teachings of Jesus and Paul.

- The link between the teachings of the New Testament and Christians today.

In the glossary

Heaven

Monk

New Testament

Nun

Paul

JESUS AND HIS TEACHING ABOUT MONEY

Jesus had as much to say about money as almost any other topic. Here are two things that he said:

A *"How hard it is to enter the kingdom of God. It is easier for a camel to go through the eye of a needle than for a rich man to enter the kingdom of God."*

Mark 10.24,25

B *"No-one can serve two masters. Either he will hate one and love the other, or he will be devoted to one and despise the other. You cannot serve both God and Money."*

Matthew 6.24

Jesus suggested that there was only one thing to do if money was getting in the way of doing God's will. He gave this piece of advice to a rich, young ruler who wanted to become a disciple:

C *"Sell everything you have and give to the poor, and you will have treasure in heaven."*

Luke 18.22

JESUS MEETS ZACCHAEUS

As Jesus was passing through the city of Jericho, he met up with Zacchaeus, a wealthy Jewish tax collector. He was wealthy because he worked for the Romans and cheated his fellow Jews. The Romans charged their taxes but Zacchaeus added his own commission on top.

The crowds were so thick around Jesus that Zacchaeus, a short man, climbed up a sycamore tree to see him. As he passed by, Jesus stopped under the tree and told Zacchaeus that he wished to visit his house for a meal. The onlookers were astonished because none of them would even dream of talking to a tax collector!

Zacchaeus was so delighted that he made an immediate promise that he would give half of his possessions to the poor and pay back four times the money that he had taken deceitfully. Jesus said to him: "Today salvation has come to this house, because this man, too, is a Son of Abraham [a Jew]. For the Son of Man [Jesus] came to seek and save what was lost." [Luke 19.9]

TAKE TIME TO THINK
The Beatles famously sang that money can't buy you love. Maybe not but can money buy you happiness?

CHRISTIANS AND MONEY TODAY

As you can imagine, Christians have never found the teaching of Jesus about money easy to put into practice. The question that everyone asks is simply this: "Did Jesus say that we should give everything away to the poor?"

In one of his letters, the Apostle Paul put a different slant on things when he wrote: "The love of money is the root of all kinds of evil. Some people, eager for money, have wandered from the faith and pierced themselves with many griefs." [1 Timothy 6.10]

Christians fall into three groups in their attitude to money:

- Some believe that Jesus had no possessions or wealth and they should follow his example. This is how **monks** and **nuns** live.
- Some believe that they only have wealth and possessions because God has given them to them. Many in this group believe that they have a duty to use their wealth wisely and generously.
- Some believe that they need some money and wealth to carry out their responsibilities. It is wrong, however, to spend all their time and energy on making themselves richer.

OVER TO YOU ▶▶▶

1 Put the three sayings of Jesus into your own words to show that you understand what he was saying.

2 Write down two reasons why you either agree or disagree with what Jesus was saying.

3 Imagine that you are a reporter working for a local radio station in Jericho. Either write down or record what you saw as Jesus met Zacchaeus.

4 Explain what you think Christians today might learn from the story of Zacchaeus.

5 Paul said that 'the love of money is the root of all kinds of evil'. Do you agree with him? Bring forward some arguments to show why you think he was right – or wrong.

WHO CARES?

You will find out

- The difference between short-term and long-term aid.

- About two Christian charities – Christian Aid and Tearfund.

In the glossary

Bible

HIV

Refugee

Aid comes in many different shapes and forms. Communities on Hatiya Island in the Bay of Bengal are severely impacted by extreme weather conditions. Tearfund's partner, Heed, is working through the local church to provide effective support.

TWO KINDS OF HELP

There are many charities working to provide help and assistance for the poorest countries. Some are Christian charities while others are non-religious. The help which they provide comes in two different forms:

- Short-term aid. When there is a natural disaster there is a quick, and very necessary, response. In Britain alone over £70 million was collected when the tsunami struck several countries in the Indian Ocean in 2004. Droughts, floods and earthquakes are much more likely to strike the poorest nations than the richest.

- Long-term aid. This is help provided over years to build up a country's hospitals, clinics, farms and schools. Long-term aid provides skilled help so that countries can learn to help themselves in the future.

A *"O God, to those who hunger give bread; and to those who have bread give the hunger for justice."*

A Latin American prayer

Here are two Christian charities which work among the poor and needy:

CHRISTIAN AID

"We believe in life before death." This motto of Christian Aid sums up the attitude of the charity. Christian Aid was started in 1954 and first worked among **refugees**. It was then extended to relief work following natural disasters – setting up different aid projects, carrying out educational work at home and overseas and campaigning for a fairer world. From Afghanistan to Brazil, Christian Aid works in some of the world's poorest communities. This is how its website describes the work that it does:

B *"Inspired by Christian values, we believe that all people have the right to a full and decent life. We don't have to accept a world in which some people have nothing and some have so much. We believe the world can change. The way we work reflects our belief that everyone deserves a full life."*

Christian Aid website

Christian Aid provides both short-term and long-term aid. It sent almost £20 million to help those affected by the tsunami. In 2005, it also provided £30 million to support long-term projects such as preventing the spread of HIV/AIDS.

You can find out more about the work of Christian Aid at www.Christian-aid.org.uk.

OVER TO **YOU** ▶▶▶

1 Explain the difference between long-term and short-term aid.

2 Make your own scrapbook of cuttings which show the differences between those who are 'haves' and those who are 'have-nots' in today's world. Add some comments of your own to show what your response is to some of the cuttings.

3 Christian Aid says that it believes the world can be changed to make it more fair. Do you and, if so, where would you start? Explain your answer and give some reasons for it.

4 Describe three of the ways that Tearfund tries to make a difference in the world.

TEARFUND

On its website, Tearfund talks about Hannah, aged 10, who wants to be a doctor because 'she wants to help people in need'. Hannah lives in a remote valley in Ethiopia and a school has just been opened in her village with support from Tearfund. This might be the beginning that Hannah needs to fulfil her dream...

Tearfund works with partners in more than 70 countries. This is how it sets about its work:

- It encourages different communities to come up with projects that will help them in the future – providing healthcare, literacy classes, clean water, HIV/AIDS education, drug rehabilitation and better crops.
- It moves very quickly when disaster strikes by providing emergency relief. It helps people who live in vulnerable places to find better ways of coping with unexpected events.
- It speaks out about the underlying causes of poverty. Tearfund depends on one verse from the Bible which gives it the authority to do this:

C *"Speak up for those who cannot speak for themselves, for the rights of all those who are destitute."*

Proverbs 31.8

- It helps people to earn their own living. This is going to be their passport out of poverty. Small loans, for example, are given to people who have the opportunity to own their own land or start a business.

You can find out more about the work of Tearfund by looking at www.tearfund.org.

TAKE TIME TO THINK

Christian Aid says that it believes in life *before* death as well as life after death. What do you think it means?

HIV AND AIDS

You will find out

- What HIV is and why it is so dangerous.
- What AIDS is.
- The Christian approach to HIV/AIDS.

In the glossary

Archbishop

HIV

People throughout the world have been warned about HIV/AIDS for over twenty years now. AIDS has already killed millions, millions continue to be infected and still there is no cure – so AIDS will kill millions more.

WHAT IS HIV?

HIV is a virus. Viruses infect the cells of living organisms and replicate [make new copies of themselves] within those cells. A virus can damage the cells it replicates in, which is one of the things that can make an infected person ill. People become infected with HIV from other people who have it, mainly through unprotected sexual intercourse.

HIV stands for 'Human Immunodeficiency Virus'. Someone who is infected with HIV is said to be 'HIV positive'.

WHY IS HIV DANGEROUS?

The immune system is a group of cells and organs that protect your body by fighting disease. The human immune system usually fights viruses fairly quickly. What makes HIV so serious is that it attacks the immune system itself – the very thing that would normally fight the virus but cannot now do so.

The person whose body has been invaded by HIV may feel perfectly well for many years and not know that they have the virus. As a person's immune system weakens, however, so they become increasingly vulnerable to other illnesses.

WHAT IS AIDS?

A damaged immune system is not only more vulnerable to HIV but also to attacks by other infections. It will not always have the strength to fight them off. As time goes by, the person who has been infected with HIV is likely to become ill more frequently until they become ill with a number of serious illnesses. It is at this point that they have AIDS. AIDS [Acquired Immune Deficiency Syndrome] is a very serious condition since the body now has little defence against any kind of infection. People die from one of these infections and not from AIDS itself.

OVER TO YOU ▶▶▶

1 If a friend asked you what HIV is, what would you say to them?

2 Write about some facts and figures which illustrate the effect that HIV/AIDS is having on Sub-Saharan Africa.

TAKE TIME TO THINK

Why do you think that Christians have been particularly concerned to help those suffering from HIV/AIDS in the last twenty years?

A CASE-STUDY – AIDS IN AFRICA

AIDS wipes out three million people – the equivalent to the population of Wales – each year. The most dramatic effect of HIV/AIDS can be seen in Africa:

- AIDS is the leading cause of death in Sub-Saharan Africa.
- During 2005, 2 million people in Sub-Saharan Africa died of illnesses brought on by AIDS.
- Nearly 65% of the world's HIV infected people live in Sub-Saharan Africa and yet the area only has 10% of the world's population. In some countries, the life expectancy is as low as 33 years of age.

In the rest of the world:

- 20 million people have died of AIDS since it was first diagnosed in the 1980s.
- 13 million people have HIV/AIDS.
- 9,000 people die each day as a result of infection with HIV/AIDS.
- 14,000 new people are infected by HIV/AIDS daily.

CHRISTIANS AND HIV/AIDS

Tearfund has made the fight against HIV/AIDS and the diseases associated with it a high priority. AIDS has created many orphans in countries such as Uganda, where whole families have been wiped out. On its website, Tearfund highlights the case of Janjho, a young girl, who managed to find £3 for a fortnight's antibiotic treatment but could not afford to pay for a full eight-month course. Tearfund supports a clinic in Janjho's area that now supplies free medication. It also provides free home visits and spiritual support to thousands of TB patients.

Tearfund also highlights some words of Jesus: "…I am come that they might have life, and have it to the full." [John 10.10] as a major motivation for its work.

Christians believe that people suffering from HIV/AIDS are often treated as lepers were treated in the time of Jesus. Archbishop Desmond Tutu, a very important Christian leader in South Africa, drew attention to this danger:

A "We should not want those living with HIV to be the modern equivalent of the Biblical leper who had to carry a bell and a sign saying 'I am unclean'. They are not unclean. We should embrace them physically and emotionally as members of our community."

Archbishop Tutu

Christians work around the world to make sure that people infected with HIV/AIDS receive the best possible medication and medical help.

FOUR THREATS TO OUR PLANET

You will find out

- About global warming and the threat it presents to our planet.

- About the ozone layer and why its destruction is a disaster.

- The importance of the world's rainforests.

- About pollution.

Our planet is under great threat from the way that we live. Here are four of the most serious threats:

THREAT 1: GLOBAL WARMING [THE GREENHOUSE EFFECT]

- Our planet is surrounded by a blanket of gases which insulates it. This blanket guarantees a steady temperature in which life can prosper.

- This blanket acts like a greenhouse around the Earth but, because of pollution, the greenhouse is becoming too warm.

- If this continues, then the ice caps in the Arctic and Antarctic will melt and water levels in the oceans of the world will rise. Many low-lying countries will be flooded.

- In the last fifty years, the snow cover on the Earth has shrunk by 10%. Massive glaciers are melting.

THREAT 2: DESTROYING THE OZONE LAYER

- Ozone in the atmosphere forms a protective layer over the Earth, filtering out the lethal ultraviolet rays from the sun.

- The use of chlorofluorocarbons from aerosols in the past has led to a hole being punched in the ozone layer. Although their use has stopped, it will take more than 100 years for the hole to be mended.

- In the meantime, people on Earth are vulnerable to a whole range of health hazards from eye cataracts to skin cancer.

Find out what recycling is and what facilities are offered in your area for the recycling of waste materials.

Pollution from cars is one of the major threats to the environment.

THREAT 3: CHOPPING DOWN THE RAINFORESTS

- Deforestation is the permanent clearing of forest areas, especially rainforests, for agriculture or building development.

- Between 1985 and 1995, forest areas were cleared at the rate of 40 million acres a year – and the rate has accelerated since then! Forests are now cleared at the rate of an area as large as Great Britain every week. An area the size of a football pitch is cleared every second!

- Deforestation makes a great contribution to global warming. Rainforests also contain 50% of the world's species – animals, plants, etc. We lose about 5,000 species a year this way. Yet many life-saving drugs are only found in forest areas.

- Rainforests prevent such disastrous events as mudslides because tree roots bind the earth together. Without them, earth can move large distances when it rains.

THREAT 4: POLLUTING THE WORLD

- There are 400 million cars in the world. By 2025, this number will almost double. Each car releases hydrocarbons from the petrol it uses. This causes all kinds of breathing problems for millions of people as well as contributing to cancer, reproductive problems and birth defects.

- Rubbish is largely placed in landfill sites but much of it does not break down – it is not biodegradable. This will pollute the world for future generations.

- Many rivers and seas of the world have lost their natural ability to clean themselves because of pollution.

- All forms of pollution have a drastic effect on wildlife. In recent years in the UK, hedgerows and wildlife meadows have been destroyed on a large scale. These places are homes to many species of wildlife. It is thought that the world loses one species of plant or animal every 15 minutes.

OVER TO YOU ▶▶▶

1 What is global warming and how do we know it is already taking place?

2 Explain why the ozone layer is so important and how we have damaged it.

3 What is meant by deforestation and why does it matter?

4 Collect some examples of threats to the environment from your newspapers and mount a wall display in your classroom under the title 'Threats to the planet'.

TAKE TIME TO THINK

In this unit, we have seen four areas in which our planet is under threat. Which of them do you find most frightening? Try to explain why.

You will find out

- About Chief Seattle and what he had to say about the environment.

- What humanists have to say about the environment.

- The work of Greenpeace.

In the glossary

Humanist

A *"Take only memories, leave nothing but footprints."*

Chief Seattle

You do not have to be religious to be concerned about the environment. Everyone is aware that the human race is polluting the planet and that time is growing very short to put things right.

CHIEF SEATTLE

Chief Seattle of the Suquamish and Duwamish Native American Tribes lived from 1786 to 1866. He lived in what is now the American State of Washington and the town of Seattle is named after him. In the beginning, he was very critical about the way that white people lived, although he soon realised that everyone, the white person and the Native American, must learn to live together with nature.

Chief Seattle left behind many memorable statements about the need of the white man to take care of the planet. Here are two of them:

B *"We know that the white man does not understand our ways. One portion of the land is the same to him as the next for he is a stranger who comes in the night and takes from the land whatever he needs. The earth is not his brother, but his enemy and when he has conquered it he moves on."*

Chief Seattle

C *"Whatever befalls the earth befalls the son of the earth. Man did not weave the web of life; he is merely a strand of it. Whatever he does to the web, he does to himself."*

Chief Seattle

HUMANISM AND THE ENVIRONMENT

Humanists are non-religious people. They do not believe in God but live on moral principles that are based on both reason and a respect for others. Humanists are concerned with human welfare and happiness. They promote human happiness in this life because they believe that it is the only life we have.

Because of their concern for human welfare and happiness, humanists care about the natural world. We all depend on this world and it will have to sustain our descendants in the future. We should care about the future of our planet because we care about other human beings – even those who are not yet born.

This is how one group of humanists see the situation:

D *"Because humanists have no belief in a god or supernatural force that will solve our problems for us, they know that human beings must take sole responsibility for sorting out our environmental problems. We are the only ones capable of finding the solutions that will lead to a sustainable future."*

Do you think that many people treat the earth as their enemy, moving on once they have conquered it?

GREENPEACE

Greenpeace is an organisation which believes in using non-violent means to protest against all threats to the environment. It began in 1971, when a small boat of volunteers sailed into Amchitka, an area north of Alaska, where the US government was conducting underground nuclear tests.

E *"Greenpeace's goal is to ensure the ability of the Earth to nurture life in all its diversity."*

Greenpeace website

To do this, Greenpeace organises public campaigns. According to its website, these campaigns are designed to:

- protect the oceans and ancient forests.
- maintain a ban on commercial whaling.
- encourage countries to look after the world's fish stocks.
- maintain a ban on mineral exploitation in Antarctica.
- fight to prevent the dumping of nuclear waste materials at sea.
- secure nuclear disarmament and the abolition of nuclear weapons.

You can find out more about Greenpeace by looking at www.greenpeace.org.uk.

OVER TO **YOU** ▶▶▶

1 Try to explain what you think Chief Seattle meant in extract A.

2 Explain why humanists believe that human beings have to solve the problems of our planet themselves.

3 Do you share the opinions expressed by humanists or not?

4 How does Greenpeace try to go about its work and what are some of the things that it is trying to achieve?

TAKE TIME TO THINK

The organisation Greenpeace believes in non-violent direct action. What do you think that this means and do you think it is a good way to achieve your objectives?

You will find out

- The creation story from the Bible.

- About the idea of dominion.

- The responsibility of human beings to be stewards of God's creation.

In the glossary

Bible

Old Testament

Steward

Here are three quotations from the Bible about creation:

A *"God blessed them [the first man and woman] and said to them, 'Be fruitful and increase in number; fill the earth and subdue it. Rule over the fish of the sea and the birds of the air and over every living creature that moves on the ground.'"*

Genesis 1.28-30

B *"O Lord, our Lord, how majestic is your name in all the earth."*

Psalm 8.1

C *"The earth is the Lord's and everything in it, the world and all who live in it."*

Psalm 24.1

By looking at extract A, it is easy to see how human beings have, for centuries, believed themselves to be at the centre of the universe. They have had an enormous impact on the world by controlling all parts of nature for their own ends. Can you imagine how different the world would be without the changes that human beings have made to it?

Three words have dominated the way that human beings have treated the world:

1: CREATION

Jews and Christians share the same creation story – found in the first three chapters of the book of Genesis. In fact, there are two creation stories:

- The seven day account of creation, building up to the creation of the first man and woman on day six, before God 'rested' on the seventh day.

- The story of Adam and Eve. Essentially the same creation story but described from the point of view of the first human beings.

OVER TO **YOU** ▶▶▶

1 Read the two stories in Genesis chapters 1, 2 and 3. Make a list of ten things which we learn from these chapters about how the world was created by God.

2 What are the two very different ways that the authority of human beings over the rest of creation can be shown?

3 Here are three aspects of nature:
   a) The environment.
   b) Human beings.
   c) All forms of life apart from human beings.
   Write down five things that being a good steward might involve in relation to each of these.

2: Dominion

The Bible speaks of human beings 'subduing' and 'ruling over' nature [A]. In the past this has been understood by Christians in two different ways:

- Human beings are given supreme power over the whole of nature to use it as they wish. If it is decided, for instance, that a new reservoir is needed then human beings have the authority to build it – whatever is destroyed in the process.

- With dominion comes responsibility. God has given human beings such responsibilities because they alone can make sure that all of God's creatures are cared for. The Old Testament tells us that: "…a righteous man cares for the needs of his animals." [Proverbs 12.10]

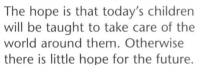
The hope is that today's children will be taught to take care of the world around them. Otherwise there is little hope for the future.

3: Stewardship

If you think about it for a moment, you might wish to argue that controlling the world, or a part of it, should mean that we are responsible for it. This idea is known as stewardship and it is an important idea in the Bible. A steward is someone who is a caretaker or a guardian and many people would argue that this best describes human beings and their role in the world. Christians believe that human beings are God's stewards, appointed by him to look after the world properly.

So what does this mean?

- Human beings, and all of nature, are part of the same web of life.

- If human beings look after the world then it will continue to look after them. There is more than enough food in the world, for example, to feed everyone if it is used properly and not wasted.

- The dependence of one part of creation on every other part is too important to ignore. Human beings need the rest of nature to be healthy to survive themselves.

You will find out

- The reasons why Christians have downgraded animals in the past.

- The attitude of the saints to animals.

- Animal-friendly thoughts which persuade Christians to treat animals kindly.

In the glossary

Monk

Old Testament

Saint

Soul

For most of history, Christians have largely ignored animal suffering. They have believed that, as human beings were far superior to animals, it didn't matter how they treated them. People had few, if any, obligations to animals.

DOWNGRADING ANIMALS

There were three main reasons why Christians had such a poor attitude to animals. They believed that:

- God had created animals solely for the benefit of human beings, who were entitled to treat them as they wished.

- Animals were inferior to human beings because God had not given them souls.

- Animals had only been put on Earth so that humans could eat them.

ANIMALS AND THE SAINTS

Not all Christians downgraded animals. Some saints were well-known for the way that they treated them. St Antony of Padua preached to the fishes. St Francis of Assisi preached to the birds and became a very popular church leader in the 13th century. Cows were protected by St Brigit. St Columba told his monks to care for a crane.

Most, if not all, of these examples of care for animals are clearly legends. What they show, however, is that many saints of the past wanted to show their followers that it was the Christian way to care for the whole of God's creation.

Much earlier than this, a writer in the Old Testament looked forward to the time when natural enemies in the animal world would live happily side by side:

A *"The wolf will live with the lamb, the leopard will lie down with the goat, the calf and the lion and the yearling together; and a little child will lead them."*

Isaiah 11.6-8

OVER TO **YOU** ▶▶▶

1 Write down your immediate reactions to these three reasons. Do you strongly agree or disagree with any of them?

2 The writer in extract A was looking forward to a perfect world in which everyone, human and animal, would live together peacefully. Could you ever imagine such a world?

3 Describe three reasons why modern Christians believe that human beings should be kind to animals.

SIX ANIMAL-FRIENDLY CHRISTIAN THOUGHTS

Here are some of the animal-friendly ideas that many modern Christians follow when thinking about animals:

Both humans and non-human animals were created by God. St Francis of Assisi said that: "...animals had the same source as himself..."

God's ideal is that human beings and animals should live together in perfect harmony as we see in extract A. The first man and woman lived peacefully together with all of creation in the Garden of Eden and this is how it should be in a perfect world.

God has the right to expect that everything he has created is treated with great respect – even the most insignificant parts of nature. As the teaching of Jesus shows, God cares for the whole of creation:

> *Are not two sparrows sold for a penny? Yet not one of them will fall to the ground apart from the will of your Father.*
>
> Matthew 10.29

Animals are weak and helpless compared with us. Christ told human beings to be kind and compassionate to those who are weaker – whether they are human or not.

To love those who cannot return that love is to act in a generous way. Jesus asked the question, "If you love them that love you what reward have you?"

It is a great good to take responsibility for the welfare of others. This includes animals.

The attitude of Christians to animals, wild and tame, has changed dramatically in recent years. Christians now believe strongly in the importance of conservation.

TAKE TIME TO THINK

a) Could you hunt and kill animals?

b) Do you think there is a difference between hunting animals for sport and hunting them for personal survival, as our ancestors needed to do?

TWO VERY TRICKY ANIMAL ISSUES

You will find out

- Whether it is right to eat animals as food or whether everyone should be a vegetarian.

- Whether it is right to use animals in laboratory experiments.

In the glossary

Bible

Vegan

Vegetarian

Vivisection

Scenes such as these have caused many people to question modern farming methods.

A "*The greatness of a nation and its moral progress can be judged by the way its animals are treated.*"

Mahatma Gandhi

In recent years, Christians and non-Christians have had to face up to two very tricky questions about the way that we treat animals. As extract A makes clear, this issue shows how much progress we have made as a nation. These two questions are:

1: SHOULD WE EAT MEAT OR NOT?

The Bible does not give Christians any clear guidance about what they should, and should not, eat. This is unlike the holy books of almost every other religion. Purely from personal preference, however, some Christians choose to be:

- **Vegetarian** – people who do not eat meat.

- **Vegan** – people who do not eat animals or animal products such as eggs.

Christians who follow one of these particular life-styles do not necessarily do so for religious reasons. Like non-religious people who make the same choice, it may simply be because they do not want to harm animals. It is much more likely, however, to be because they disagree strongly with some modern farming methods such as keeping hens in cages or rearing calves in crates.

Others think that vegetables, especially if they are grown organically, are safer to eat than meat or animal products. In the last decade or two, scares such as salmonella in eggs and BSE in cattle have caused many people to question seriously what they are eating. This said, however, meat still forms a major source of protein for most people.

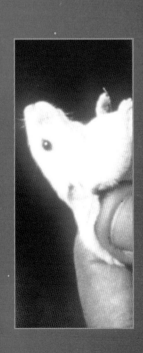

2: SHOULD WE USE ANIMALS IN SCIENTIFIC EXPERIMENTS?

Using animals in carefully controlled scientific experiments is called vivisection. Many medical advances in the 20th century came about after experiments on animals. Such experimentation was used for the development of insulin for diabetes as well as vaccines against whooping cough, diphtheria, rubella and polio.

Here is a dictionary definition of vivisection: "The cutting up of live animals."

The word now covers all scientific experiments on animals. Are they right or wrong? Before making your mind up, think about the following:

Against vivisection: Things are now changing. Animals are now rarely used for the testing of new cosmetics and other commercial products. Things changed some time ago when The Body Shop and other shops announced that they would not stock products tested on animals.

The BUAV [British Union for the Abolition of Vivisection] argues that all such experiments are unnecessary. There are now alternatives – such as artificial cells and tissues – which make experiments on animals unnecessary.

For vivisection: The vast majority of scientists and doctors believe that animal experiments are still necessary. They point out that less than 3,000,000 a year are now carried out – although this figure is still rising year by year. 85% of these are carried out on rodents – rats and mice. Tests may not be the same on animals and humans but they are close enough to yield some very valuable information. At the moment, scientists are investigating the use of animal organs for human transplants.

Most Christians would support the use of animals in scientific experiments if it benefits the human race. All of the other world religions would agree with this conclusion.

> The use of animals in scientific experiments is increasing and scientists argue that this is still necessary in the battle against illness and disease.

OVER TO YOU ▶▶▶

1 Do you think that animals should be used for food? Are some sources of meat more acceptable to you than others?

2 Do you think that people should make enquiries about how their food is produced before they buy it? Does it matter to you?

3 Explain the difference between a vegetarian and a vegan. Give some reasons why a person might avoid eating meat.

4 Most Christians support the use of animals in scientific experiments if the human race benefits and cures are found for the many killer diseases. Do you agree? List the arguments for and against.

You will find out

- About a meeting of the world's religious leaders to discuss nature.

- About the Sacred Lands Project.

- About the Sacred Orchid Project.

In the glossary

Altar

Saint

In 1986, HRH Prince Philip, then President of the Worldwide Fund for Nature International, issued an invitation. He asked leaders of five major world religions – Christianity, Judaism, Islam, Buddhism and Hinduism – to meet with him to discuss how they could help to save the natural world. He called them to Assisi because this is a town associated with St Francis, a saint famous for his love of nature.

It was an extraordinary event. For the first time, religious leaders met with representatives of the major charities concerned with saving the planet. Prince Philip said:

A "*If you believe in God – which is what Christians are supposed to do – then you should feel a responsibility to care for his creation.*"

Prince Philip

The mood of the meeting was captured in the words of welcome:

B "*Each religion will celebrate the dignity of nature and the duty of every person to live harmoniously within the natural world… We are humble enough to desire to learn from each other. The very richness of our diversity lends strength to our shared concern and responsibility for Planet Earth.*"

Father Serrini of the Franciscan Order

By 1995, four other religions – the Baha'is, the Daoists, the Sikhs and the Jains – had joined the original five religions. The Alliance of Religions and Conservation [ARC] was born. Here are just two sides of its work:

THE SACRED LANDS PROJECT

There are many sacred pilgrimage sites in the major world religions. In Britain, a project was launched to tell people that the land where they live can be as sacred as holy sites elsewhere. Christians, Jews, Hindus, Muslims and non-religious organisations were involved in a series of projects:

CHECK IT OUT

created and revived inner-city community gardens.

conserved and celebrated holy wells.

celebrated sacred places with works of art and poems.

The Sacred Lands Project has...

rediscovered and renewed old pilgrimage trails.

protected trees and woodlands.

Sacred Lands is the WWF's major religious project in Britain. It has the backing of the principal Churches and all major religious faiths practised in Britain.

SACRED ORCHID PROJECT

This work began in Mexico in 2006. The project is to work with villagers in remote areas of Mexico to conserve rare and endangered species of plants – especially those used in religious ceremonies. Here are two examples:

- **Palms.** Used throughout the Catholic world not only on Palm Sunday but also for weddings, funerals and other occasions. They are harvested in forests in Southern Mexico and yet many young plants are wasted and destroyed.

- **Orchids.** These are widely used as altar offerings and church decorations in Mexico. A special orchid garden has been set up in which over 500 rare species are preserved. This educates villagers about the importance of looking after the environment.

The world's religions are responsible for a vast amount of land and much of this could be turned into nature reserves as well as places of worship and pilgrimage. It is one of the purposes of ARC to encourage this.

OVER TO **YOU** ▶▶▶

1 What do you think is meant by 'the dignity of nature' and how do you think it can be celebrated?

2 Do you think that you live in harmony with nature? Think of some examples to show that you do. Think of some examples to show that you don't.

3 Explain some of the objectives of the Sacred Lands Project.

4 Describe three places of worship in your area that you know. How do you think they could be used as nature reserves as well as places of worship?

Gardens in inner city areas bring people a great deal of peace and space to unwind.

TAKE TIME TO THINK

Do you think that people would benefit from having areas for quiet and reflection close to them – even in the inner city?

WARS, WARS AND STILL MORE WARS

You will find out

- About war during the 20th century.

- Some of the reasons why nations go to war.

- A warning from Jesus.

In the glossary

Refugee

War, and the use of military aggression, is one of the greatest problems facing the human race. It is staggering to realise that more people died in the wars in the 20th century than in all other centuries in history added together.

CHECK IT OUT

In the 20th century, more than 100 million people died in armed conflict.

About 9 million died in battle in the First World War.

Now over 90% of casualties are civilians.

Wars in the 20th century

62 million died in the Second World War.

In the First World War, 95% of casualties were soldiers.

Over 21 million were injured in the First World War.

5 times as many people were injured as killed.

Jesus was very pessimistic about the possibility of wars ever ending. Do you share his pessimism or are you more hopeful?

WHY DO PEOPLE FIGHT?

Apart from the death and injuries, modern warfare inflicts suffering on a far wider scale. It deprives millions of people of their homes, turning them into refugees. Here is one example. When the Russian army moved into Afghanistan in 1979, thousands were made homeless. By the time it left, ten years later, over 50% of the population had become refugees. Hospitals, schools, businesses and water supplies were disrupted or destroyed.

Why, then, do people fight when the cost is so high? Several people were asked for their opinions:

> Different political groups within a country may violently disagree with each other. Their disagreement may be so strong that they fight. Often one side may see itself as fighting 'a war of liberation' against the government.

> A country may have a disagreement with another over a disputed border. Sometimes the dispute may be over a stretch of water rather than land. Valuable commodities like oil or gas may be at the heart of the dispute.

> One country may lay claim to another and that leads to a war.

> People may think that a war is the only way open to them to solve a dispute with another country.

> From time to time, dictators take power in a country by force. They have to be resisted – even if that involves another country intervening.

OVER TO YOU ▶▶▶

1   Can you explain why the 20th century was known as the 'bloody century'?

2   Think of two wars about which you have some knowledge. Write a paragraph explaining why they were fought. Did they end up solving the problem?

3   Can you ever see a time coming when war will be a thing of the past and different nations will find other ways of solving their problems? Before you form your answer, look at Isaiah 11.6 and decide whether this verse has anything to say.

TAKE TIME TO THINK

Jesus suggested that there would never be a time when the world would be free from war and violence. He said:

A "You will hear of wars and rumours of wars, but see to it that you are not alarmed. Such things must happen but the end is still to come."

Matthew 24.6,7

IS THE BIBLE A BOOK OF PEACE?

You will find out

- The teaching of the Old Testament about war and peace.
- The teaching of Jesus about war and peace.
- How the actions of Jesus supported his teaching.

In the glossary

Beatitudes

Bible

Heaven

Old Testament

Peter

Prophet

Ten Commandments

You would expect the Bible to be a book of peace, but is it? To decide, think about:

Jesus had much to say about the ways that people can live together in peace.

1: THE OLD TESTAMENT

Here are four quotations from the Old Testament. They seem to present contradictory evidence about the attitude of the Jewish Scriptures towards war and violence.

This is one of the Ten Commandments:

A "*You shall not murder.*"

Exodus 20.13

Extract B suggests that there is a time when people should seek peace – and a time when they must go to war:

B "*There is a time for everything, and a season for every activity under heaven… a time to love and a time to hate, a time for war and a time for peace…*"

Ecclesiastes 3.3,8

When the Israelites, the Jews, left slavery in Egypt, they travelled towards the country that God had promised to give them. On the way, they had to fight against tribes who already occupied the land. Some of the battles were ruthless and bloody.

Here is the description of one such encounter:

> *When Israel had finished killing all the men of Ai in the fields and in the desert where they had chased them, and when every one of them had been put to the sword. All the Israelites returned to Ai and killed those who were in it. Twelve thousand men and women fell that day... as the Lord had instructed Joshua.*
>
> Joshua 8.24,25,28

Others, though, were not sure about the wisdom of all this war. One Jewish **prophet**, Micah, told the people that, in future, God would solve their disputes and they should turn their swords into ploughs and their spears into pruning knives! In other words, they should become a people of peace not war!

2: THE TEACHING OF JESUS

Perhaps the most important teaching of Jesus is found in a series of statements called the **Beatitudes**. In them, Jesus said:

> *...blessed are the peacemakers for they will be called the sons of God.*
>
> Matthew 5.9

Jesus promised that he would leave his own peace with his followers and one of the favourite titles given to Jesus was that of the Prince of Peace. He also gave this piece of advice to his disciples:

> *You have heard that it was said, 'Love your neighbour and hate your enemy'. But I tell you: Love your enemies and pray for those who persecute you.*
>
> Matthew 5.43

TAKE TIME TO THINK

If Jesus was on Earth today and one of his followers was thinking seriously about becoming a soldier, what do you think he would say?

3: THE ACTIONS OF JESUS

There are several things for you to consider:

Just before his arrest, Jesus advised his disciples to sell their cloaks so that they could buy a sword. [Luke 22.36]

When Jesus found people trading in the Temple, he overturned their tables and drove them from the Temple with a whip. [John 2.15,16]

When Jesus was arrested, one of his followers, probably **Peter**, cut off the ear of the servant of the High Priest. Jesus told him to put the sword back in its sheath since: "...all who draw the sword will die by the sword..." [Matthew 26.52] He then healed the man's ear.

During his trial before Pontius Pilate, the Roman governor, many accusations were levelled against Jesus but he: "...refused to say a word and Pilate was amazed." [Mark 15.5]

OVER TO **YOU** ▶▶▶

1 You have been asked to give a class talk with the title 'What does the Old Testament have to say about war?' What would you say?

2 Describe the teaching of Jesus about war and violence.

3 Find out the meaning of the word 'pacifism'.

4 Do you think that it would be accurate to describe Jesus as a pacifist from what you know of his words and actions?

5 Did Jesus encourage his followers to be pacifists?

IS IT PEACE OR IS IT WAR?

You will find out

- The idea of fighting a Just War – is it possible?
- About pacifism.

In the glossary

Anglican Church

Just War

Pacifism

Quakers

Roman Catholic Church

·STAY·
·AND·REMEMBER·
·THOSE·WHO·DIED·
·FOR·YOU·

Why do you think that so many people in society are opposed to pacifism?

When Christians are forced to choose between fighting in a war or not, there are two main points of view:

OVER TO **YOU** ▶▶▶

1 How would you explain to someone else the meaning of the phrase 'a Just War'?
2 What conditions need to be met for a war to be considered 'just'?
3 What is pacifism?
4 Explain why some Christians might refuse to fight in a war.
5 Look at the Quaker Peace Pledge. Put it into your own words to show that you understand what is being said.

THE JUST WAR

No-one enjoys fighting in a war. Christians, like many non-Christians, believe that they should go to almost any length before a war is declared. Many Christians, however, believe that there are occasions when there is no alternative. The Second World War, when the world was threatened by the dictator, Adolf Hitler, is usually held up as the supreme example of this.

It is in situations like these that many Christians speak of a **Just War**. For a war to be 'just', certain conditions must be met:

- The war must be fought for a just cause, e.g. a country may be defending itself against an aggressor.
- The war must be fought to achieve good ends. When these goals have been reached, peace must be declared.
- The war must be declared by a legitimate authority, i.e. the government of a country.
- Every other alternative to war must be explored first, e.g. negotiation.
- The war must be fought in a just way. This means that:
  - certain weapons which cause great destruction must not be used. This would rule out, for example, the use of nuclear weapons.
  - only as much force as is needed to achieve victory should be used.
  - no violence must be directed specifically against civilians.

The Roman Catholic and the Anglican Churches support the idea of a Just War. One recent book written by a Roman Catholic argues that a Just War can only be waged if:

A *"...it is the only way of restraining a very great injustice; will not itself bring about greater destruction than the evil it opposes; has a reasonable chance of success; does not involve the deliberate killing of civilians and that those who wage it are authorised to do so by a large degree of popular support..."*

PACIFISM

For the first three centuries of its existence, few members of the Christian Church joined the Roman army. They knew only too well the teaching of Jesus of which this is an example:

B *"If someone strikes you on the right cheek, turn to him the other also."*
Matthew 5.39

The approach of Jesus here is known as **pacifism**. It was only when the Roman Emperor Constantine became a Christian at the start of the 4th century that Christians began to join the army in large numbers and pacifism went out of fashion.

Not all Christians are pacifists. Not all pacifists are Christians. Those who are Christians base their objection to any form of violence on many of the words and actions of Jesus which we mentioned in unit 45.

Only one branch of the Christian Church is officially pacifist and that is the Quakers. This group, founded in 1652, has been committed to peace and reconciliation ever since. In 1660, they handed over a declaration to King Charles II, in which they made their beliefs very clear.

C *"We utterly deny all outward wars and strife; and fighting with outward weapons, for any end, or under any pretence whatsoever; this is our testimony to the whole world. The Spirit of Christ by which we are guided is not changeable, so at once to command us from a thing as evil, and again to move unto it; and we certainly know, and testify to the world that the Spirit of Christ, which leads us into all truth will never move us to fight and war against any man with outward weapons, neither for the Kingdom of Christ, nor for the kingdoms of this world."*
Quaker Peace Pledge, 1660

95

CHRISTIAN WORKERS FOR WORLD PEACE

You will find out

- About Christian CND.
- About Quaker Peace and Social Action.
- About The Fellowship of Reconciliation.

In the glossary

Pacifism

Quakers

If you feed 'Peace Organisations' into the search engine on your computer, you will come up with a very long list. Look at the list closely and you will find that many of them are religious organisations, of which a sizeable number represent different Christian groups and denominations. In this unit, we will look at three of these organisations:

CHRISTIAN CND

The Campaign for Nuclear Disarmament has been around since the 1950s. As its name suggests, it works for the abolition of all nuclear weapons in the world. Christian CND brings a Christian emphasis to the same demand. Its motto is: "Christians working and praying for a nuclear weapons free world."

Christian CND believes that:

- nuclear weapons are evil.
- the wholesale destruction threatened by such weapons is an offence against God.
- Christian belief in and worship of God challenges possession of nuclear weapons.
- it is better to trust in God than nuclear weapons.
- Christians should cooperate with anyone who works for the abolition of nuclear weapons.

Christian CND calls on people of different faiths, and no religious faith, to join it in its mission.

QUAKER PEACE AND SOCIAL ACTION

The Quakers are a Christian Church which believes that the creative power of God is found in every human being. Quaker Peace and Social Action works to bring about peace and justice in the world through non-violent action. Quakers are pacifists.

Turning the Tide works with non-violent groups throughout the world. Among other groups, it has worked with peace groups in Palestine and Israel and the Iona Community in Scotland. You can find out more about Turning the Tide from http://www.turning-the-tide.org/.

A *"You cannot foster harmony by the apparatus of discord, nor cherish goodwill by the equipment of hate. But it is by harmony and goodwill that human security can be obtained."*

Quaker Faith and Practice 24.40

The dove has been adopted by more than one Christian peace organisation as a symbol of peace.

The first dropping of an atomic bomb took place in Japan in 1945 to hasten the end of the Second World War. Since then, many nations have acquired atomic weapons.

THE FELLOWSHIP OF RECONCILIATION

The Fellowship of Reconciliation believes that all Christians are called to be peacemakers wherever God has called them to be. It was formed in the days following the outbreak of the First World War in 1914, when it seemed that the whole world was in danger of falling apart. Two Christians, an Englishman and a German, parted company on Cologne Station with the words: "We are believers in Christ and can never be at war."

From the beginning, it has taught that the message of peace lies at the heart of the teachings of Jesus. The same message is needed in the modern world more than ever.

OVER TO **YOU** ▶▶▶

1   We hear very little these days about nuclear weapons – and their great power. How much do you know?

2   The challenge of Quakers is that life could be transformed if every person refused to use violence both individually and in society generally. Do you think this could work in everyday life? Give one or two examples of the difference it might make.

3   Find out more information about two of the Christian peace organisations for which you have the website in this unit. Write up some information about the goals of the organisations and how they try to achieve them.

CHECK IT OUT

Anglican Pacifist Fellowship – www.anglicancommunion.org

Unitarian Peace Fellowship – www.uupf.org

Four Christian peace organisation

Pax Christi – www.paxchristi.org.uk

World Peace Prayer Fellowship – www.worldpeace.org

97

RELIGIONS FOR PEACE

You will find out

- About Religions for Peace.
- About the Week of Prayer for World Peace.

A *"Today, our religions are being hijacked by religious extremists, unscrupulous politicians, and by the sensationalist media. If to hijack is to seize control of a vehicle of transport - a plane, a bus, an automobile - and to hold its passengers hostage; then our vehicles of faith, our religions are being hijacked, and we as a human family are being held against our will. Our vehicles of faith must be rescued from the hijackers' grasp. Respecting our differences, pooling our collective moral strengths and building an alliance for peace is the way we can rescue our vehicles of faith."*

Dr. William F. Vendley, Secretary General, Religions for Peace

In unit 47, you found out about three Christian peace organisations. Many Christians believe, however, that if real peace is ever going to be reached then all of the major faiths need to work together.

Religions for Peace was founded in 1970 to harness religious communities throughout the world in a search for peace. These communities claim the allegiance of billions of believers. They bridge the divides of race and class. They alone are capable of resolving conflicts, caring for the sick and promoting peace among peoples.

THE WORK OF RELIGIONS FOR PEACE

CHECK IT OUT

Some recent successes of Religions for Peace

- Launching a programme to help children affected by AIDS in Africa through the Hope for African Children Initiative.
- Bringing together warring factions in the Middle East.
- Bringing together the world's religious leaders every 5 years.
- Creating an opportunity for dialogue among different parties from such troubled areas as Iraq, Sudan, Sri Lanka, and the Korean Peninsula.
- Organising an international network of women's and youth groups.
- Helping to achieve reconciliation in Bosnia and Kosovo.

WEEK OF PRAYER FOR WORLD PEACE

Each year different religions organise a Week of Prayer for World Peace. This has been held since 1974, when its early leader declared that:

B *"Prayer for world peace has to be offered by the world's faiths..."*

Each year, a group representing the Baha'i, Buddhist, Christian, Hindu, Jain, Jewish, Muslim, Sikh and Zoroastrian faiths puts forward prayers and readings to be used by those taking part. Members of peace groups and faith communities take part in services in different parts of the country.

Here are some prayers and readings from the 2004 Week of Prayer for World Peace:

C *"Do not fear. He who fears, hates. He who hates, kills. Break the sword and throw it away."*

Mahatma Gandhi

"May peace triumph over discord."

Zoroastrian

"May it please You to bless all peoples at all times and in all places with Your gift of peace."

Jewish

During this week, people were encouraged to pray, among other things, for:

- People who have been tragically wounded in conflicts throughout the world.

- People who are taught to have bitterness toward others.

- Nations and individuals with scores to settle.

- Those who cannot allow themselves to forgive.

- Those who are unable to let themselves be forgiven.

You can find out about the most recent Week of Prayer for World Peace by looking at: http://nfpb.gn.apc.org.

OVER TO **YOU** ▶▶▶

1 Why do many people think that members of different religious faiths should be in the forefront of those working for world peace?

2 Do you agree?

3 Look carefully at the prayers from different religions on this page. Imagine that you have been asked to organise a Week of Prayer for World Peace for people of all religious faiths. Compose a prayer which could be used by people of any religion. Draw up a list of five items in the modern world that you would like to encourage people to pray for.

TAKE TIME TO THINK

Do you think that praying for world peace can make any difference? Explain your answer, whatever it is.

WHAT IS SUFFERING?

Sickness and suffering are amongst the most serious problems that believers in God have to face – including Christians. Sickness brings everyone face to face with their own mortality and powerlessness. As the Catechism of the Catholic Church says:

A *"Every illness can make us glimpse death."*

There are two kinds of suffering:

SUFFERING DUE TO NATURAL CAUSES

Much suffering is not man-made. It is not anyone's fault. It is due to natural causes. The television and the newspapers regularly bring into our homes pictures of earthquakes, floods and mudslides which kill thousands and destroy the homes of many more. Two things need to be said about these 'natural disasters':

- They usually hit the poorest and most vulnerable members of society. This is often because it is these people who live in areas which are most vulnerable to swift changes in nature or the weather.

- Although a large natural disaster does make people in other parts of the world feel helpless, there is usually a very swift response. One of the worst natural disasters in recent years, the tsunami which hit countries in the Indian Ocean on Boxing Day 2004, led to people donating over £70 million in the UK alone.

Some people might want to hold God to blame for the natural suffering in the world. After all, they argue, God made the world the way it is. He could prevent droughts, floods and earthquakes but doesn't.

MAN-MADE SUFFERING

Much of the suffering in today's world is caused by the actions of men and women. Here are four examples:

- A person drinks too much alcohol, drives a car into a pedestrian and kills them. The unhappiness they cause the person's family cannot be measured – and all because of their selfishness.

- A person smokes 40 cigarettes a day for 30 years and suffers from lung cancer. Doctors have no doubt that the cancer was the direct result of the smoking.

- A country goes to war and thousands are killed. Many more, mainly civilians, are injured. Houses are flattened. Water supplies are destroyed. The suffering is immeasurable.

- A man becomes addicted to drugs. He breaks up his family and turns to crime to finance his drug habit.

All of these examples of suffering are very sad. Who, though, do you hold responsible?

A PROBLEM TO THOSE WHO BELIEVE IN GOD

Many more examples of suffering could be given. It is not just the 'fact' of suffering which causes problems but the 'unfairness' of it all. Millions of people have never known a minute free from suffering. Others have rarely suffered.

Why does suffering happen? Is there some overall purpose behind life? Is life meaningful or meaningless? These are questions that a Christian cannot avoid. In the end it all boils down to a simple equation:

> Either God does want to remove suffering but he cannot – in which case he cannot be all-powerful.

OR

> God can remove suffering but chooses not to do so – in which case he cannot be all-good and all-loving.

You will find out more about this 'impossible equation' in units 51 and 52.

Natural disasters like this are all too frequent. They shake the faith that many people have in God.

OVER TO YOU ▶▶▶

1 Write down as many natural disasters as you can think of which have taken place in your lifetime. Do you think that anyone might have been to blame for any of them?

2 Do you think that God can be held responsible for the natural suffering in the world?

3 Describe three examples of suffering which you think are particularly difficult to explain.

TAKE TIME TO THINK

Look at the dilemma that we have posed above. What do you personally think that the answer to it might be?

WHAT ABOUT EVIL AND SUFFERING?

You will find out

- The nature of evil.

- The idea that suffering is a punishment.

- The first 'sin' – that of Adam and Eve.

In the glossary

Bible

Old Testament

Prophet

Satan

Sin

WHAT IS EVIL?

This question raises many other questions:

- Are natural disasters – such as earthquakes and hurricanes – that kill thousands and leave immense destruction behind them evil?

- Are infamous dictators such as Adolph Hitler and Saddam Hussein evil?

- Was someone like Thomas Hamilton, who slaughtered many children and a teacher in a school in Dunblane in 1996, evil? The headmaster of the school certainly thought so. He said: "Evil visited our school today."

Many people are quite sure that evil exists and that it is active in today's world. Each of the examples above brought untold, and unnecessary, suffering to innocent people. Evil and suffering seem to be very closely linked.

The story of creation in the Bible suggests that sin entered the world through the actions of the first woman, Eve.

SUFFERING AS PUNISHMENT

People have suffered since the beginning of time. In the days of the Old Testament, the Jews certainly suffered. They spent, for instance, over 400 years in Egyptian slavery, during which time they were treated very cruelly. We are told that God often sent his messengers to the Jews to tell them that they were suffering because they had broken his laws. These men and women were called prophets. They called on the people to repent of their sins.

God was the author of their suffering. The Old Testament teaches, however, that the Jews only had themselves to blame because they disobeyed God time and time again. This story is acted out throughout the Jewish Scriptures.

There are some people today who still believe that they, or other people, are suffering because of the sins they have committed.

OVER TO **YOU** ▶▶▶

1 Do you think that there is such a thing as evil?

2 Do you think that each of these examples shows that evil is alive and active in today's world or is there another explanation for them?

3 The story of Adam and Eve suggests that all evil comes from a single source – Satan. Do you think that there is a power of evil in the world?

THE SIN IN THE GARDEN

There is another explanation in the Bible for sin and evil in the world. You can read it for yourself in Genesis chapter 3.

In the story, God has created everything and placed the first man and woman, Adam and Eve, in a perfect garden. He leaves them with the instruction that they can eat everything in the garden *apart from* the fruit of the tree of the knowledge of good and evil standing in the middle of the garden.

After some time, Eve was tempted by a snake [called 'a serpent'] to eat the fruit and she persuaded Adam to follow her example. God was furious that they had disobeyed him and threw them out of the garden. Adam was punished for his disobedience by having to work hard to provide food for his family. Eve was punished by having to suffer the pain of childbirth – as would all women.

Few people believe this story to be literally true. It has, however, affected the way that we think about evil:

- The snake has become a powerful symbol for evil.

- Some Christians believe that the sinful action of Eve has affected all human beings ever since. Everyone now has a tendency to commit sin from the moment they are born. This belief is called 'Original Sin'.

- Some Christians believe that all evil comes from the Devil [the tempter], who is the symbol of evil in the world. Christians and Jews know the Devil as Satan. Satan is the source of all suffering in the world.

TAKE TIME TO THINK

What do you make of the story of Adam and Eve? Could it be literally true? Could it be making some important points about human nature and the way that people behave? If so, what are those points?

CAN THERE BE A GOD IF THERE IS SUFFERING?

You will find out

- An imaginary conversation between two friends.

- Suggested reasons why suffering takes place.

- About free will.

In the glossary

Free Will

Satan

At the end of unit 49, we posed one of the most difficult of all the 'ultimate questions'. We asked how people can continue to believe in God when they see so much suffering all around them. This is not a new question and all of the world faiths supply their own answers to it.

AN IMAGINARY CONVERSATION

This is the kind of conversation that you might have with one of your friends – in one of your more serious moments!

Alan: I have always believed in God – at least for as long as I can remember. I still do.

Anne: When I was young, I believed in God, but that was before I began to think seriously about the matter. Things changed for me when my auntie was killed in a car crash a few years ago. She left behind a husband and two young children. My faith in God died that day.

Alan: That is very sad, but why did you blame God? God does not promise us that we will be kept safe from all the unpleasant things of life. Only that he will be with us if they affect us and we will not be left alone.

Anne: That may satisfy you but it is not good enough for me. Christians expect me to believe in an almighty God who protects and cares for me. How can I do that after what happened to my auntie?

WHY SUFFERING?

Christians probably give more thought to this question than any other. Here are some of the answers that they have come up with:

- Suffering is God's way of allowing a person's religious faith to be tested. Suffering can deepen that faith. Problem: Is it God that does the testing or some other power? As well as deepening a person's faith, suffering can also destroy it.

- Suffering is caused by some power of evil – which Christians called Satan. Problem: Just how powerful is Satan? Less powerful than God? As powerful as God? More powerful than God? Why does God not destroy this power so that suffering and evil can end?

- Suffering brings out the best in people, whether they are actually suffering or see someone else suffering. Suffering makes people care. Problem: Surely there are other ways to bring out the best qualities in people? Is it right that someone should suffer so that my best qualities can come to the surface?

- Suffering cannot be blamed on God, it is usually the fault of people. Problem: This is not true for much of the suffering that people undergo.

WHAT ABOUT FREE WILL?

Many people put forward the following as an explanation for the suffering that there is in the world. See what you think:

- When God created human beings, he gave them freedom to make their own choices. This is called 'free will'.

- If we have 'free will' then we must be able to make important choices for ourselves. The most important of these choices are the 'ultimate questions' at which we have been looking.

- If we are free to make these choices then we must take the consequences of our actions.

- The consequences of our choices can be either good or bad. The bad consequences of our actions may involve suffering.

- If people want to have free will, they cannot hold God responsible for the unpleasant things in life. The alternative is to be little more than a puppet with God pulling the strings.

There are two problems here. We may make the right choice and use our free will properly – and still suffer as a consequence. We may also suffer because matters are completely beyond our control.

OVER TO **YOU** ▶▶▶

1 Develop the conversation between Alan and Anne further to show how you think it might end.

2 What answers do you think a Christian might give to the questions raised by Anne?

3 Look at these different explanations carefully. Do you find any, or all, of them convincing? Give reasons for your answer. Perhaps you can suggest another explanation?

Anyone who believes in God must ask the question, why was this man born blind?

HOW DO CHRISTIANS COPE WITH SUFFERING?

You will find out

- The way that Christians respond to self-inflicted suffering.

- The way that Christians respond to natural disasters.

- The Christian approach to suffering.

In the glossary

Anointing the Sick

Heaven

Hospice

Roman Catholic Church

Sacrament

Sin

How do Christians respond to the suffering around them?

CHRISTIANS AND SELF-INFLICTED SUFFERING

Look carefully at these two very different opinions:

> If people bring suffering on themselves, they must take the consequences. They cannot expect other people to help them out of the hole that they have dug for themselves. That is not how the real world works.

Thomas

> In the end, it does not matter why people are suffering. If you are a real human being, and you see someone suffering, you simply have to do something to help. It does not matter why that person is suffering – whether it is their own fault or not.

Julie

These are two very different approaches to suffering here. One of them puts forward a Christian approach and the other does not. Most people would find Thomas' approach to be unkind and cruel. Julie, on the other hand, is putting forward an opinion that Christians – and many non-Christians – would share. There is only one thing to do when you come across suffering – roll up your sleeves and do something to help – without asking any questions.

CHRISTIANS AND NATURAL DISASTERS

Christians do not believe that God can be blamed for natural disasters. Often such disasters are the result of poor decision-making. Here is an example:

> Remember the Aberfan disaster in Wales in 1966. A coal-tip engulfed a school, killing over one hundred children. The enquiry made it clear that people knew that underground streams were making the tip unsafe – and that no-one did anything about it. Given that, who do you hold responsible. God? Surely not!

Wynne

> Christians believe that Jesus has left them with the perfect example of how to accept suffering.

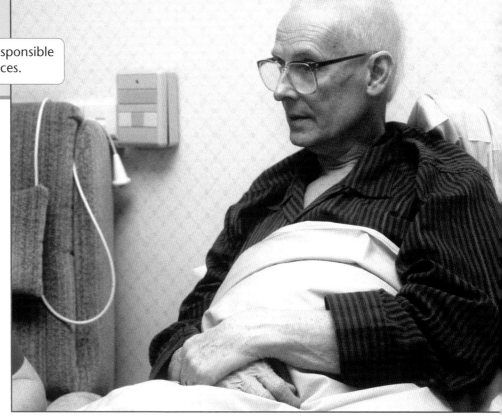

Christians have been responsible for starting many hospices.

WHAT DO CHRISTIANS SAY?

At the heart of the Christian faith is the story of Jesus, the Son of God, who lived as a genuine human being before meeting a violent death. Jesus suffered a great deal because his death was necessary so that God could forgive the sins of the human race.

This is why Christians find in Jesus a Saviour who can understand, and share in, their sufferings.

OVER TO **YOU** ▶▶▶

1   Explain why you think that either Thomas' or Anne's opinion expresses how a Christian feels about suffering while the other does not.

2   Express your own opinion about how we should treat people who are suffering because of something they have done.

3   Hospices are a very important way of helping many people to cope with suffering and death. Find out a little more about them. You will find some helpful information on:

www.childrenhospice.org   www.hospiceinformation.org

TAKE TIME TO THINK

How do you think a Christian who is suffering might draw comfort from the suffering of Jesus?

Because Jesus rose from the dead after three days, Christians also look forward to the time, in heaven, when sickness will no longer exist. Extract A expresses this hope of heaven:

A   " … [in heaven] God's home is with human beings! He will live with them… and He will be their God. God Himself will be with them, and He will be their God. He will wipe away all tears from their eyes. There will be no more death, no more grief or crying or pain. The old things have disappeared."

Revelation 21.3-4

Christians pray that God will be with those who suffer and heal them. Christians have always been in the forefront of those trying to bring comfort and healing to those who suffer in hospitals and **hospices**. Anointing the Sick with oil is one of the sacraments carried out by the Roman Catholic Church.

IS LIFE SACRED?

You will find out

- The way that moral decisions are made.

- Two very important moral issues.

- About the sanctity of life.

- The Golden Rule.

In the glossary

Abortion

Roman Catholic Church

MAKING MORAL DECISIONS

As you will have found out already, we all have many important moral decisions to make as we move through life from birth to death. Some decisions will be comparatively straightforward while others will be much more difficult. As we make each decision, we will need to take many things into account:

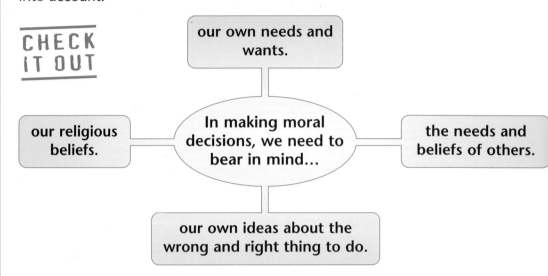

CHECK IT OUT

In making moral decisions, we need to bear in mind…

- our own needs and wants.
- the needs and beliefs of others.
- our own ideas about the wrong and right thing to do.
- our religious beliefs.

Moral decisions are rarely easy to make because of everything that we need to bear in mind.

TWO LIFE ISSUES

Here are two life issues which you will have considered before you reach the end of this book. Both of them raise the issue of whether there is something sacred or holy about life – as most religious people believe.

1 Abortion. This is the decision that a pregnant girl or woman has to make if she wants that pregnancy to end. By its very nature, this is a question that raises all kinds of other questions. Because it is a very personal decision, a person may find it very difficult to talk it over with someone else – or accept their advice.

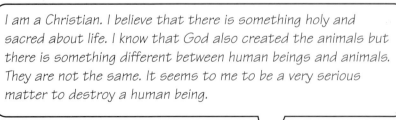

I am a Christian. I believe that there is something holy and sacred about life. I know that God also created the animals but there is something different between human beings and animals. They are not the same. It seems to me to be a very serious matter to destroy a human being.

Jackie

You will look at abortion in units 54 and 55.

2 War. Inevitably, war involves the taking of life. This is what those who fight in a war are trained to do. We looked at war in units 44-48.

THE SANCTITY OF LIFE

Most Christians believe that life is sacred. Wherever it is found, it is created by God. This is why all of the Christian Churches, and especially the Roman Catholic Church, are opposed to abortion. This is stated very clearly in extract A:

A "*God alone is the lord of life from its beginning to end: no one can under any circumstances, claim for himself directly to destroy an innocent human being.*"

Catechism of the Catholic Church, 2258

The Church would use the same argument against war as against abortion.

THE GOLDEN RULE

How, then, do Christians believe that they should treat other human beings?

> *I have always believed as a Christian that I should follow the Golden Rule that Jesus gave to his disciples. He told them that they should love their neighbour as they loved themselves. Most of us find it pretty easy to love ourselves. In fact, most of us are completely in love with ourselves. Loving our neighbour as much, however, is rather difficult...*

Peter

Christians believe that all life is sacred.

OVER TO YOU ▶▶▶

1 Here are two important moral decisions that you might have to make at some time in the future:

   a) Should I live a simpler life so that I can support others who have very little?

   b) Should I change my life-style so that I can play my part in saving the planet?

   Working with a partner, work out how you would go about reaching a decision on these two important issues.

2 Do you think that there is something holy and sacred about human life? Explain your answer, whatever it is.

3 Do you think that human beings and animals are different? If so, what is it that makes human beings special?

You will find out

- What an abortion is.
- The law about abortion.
- When life might begin.

In the glossary

Abortion

Roman Catholic Church

Soul

An abortion is the deliberate removal of a growing foetus from a woman's womb using a surgical procedure. A spontaneous abortion [called a miscarriage] takes place if the body expels the foetus naturally from the womb, usually because there is something wrong with it.

ABORTION – THE LAW

Before 1967, all abortions in England and Wales were illegal. In that year, abortion became legal as long as:

CHECK IT OUT

An abortion is legal in the UK as long as…

- the pregnancy puts the mother's life at risk.
- giving birth would endanger the mental health of the mother.
- there is a real risk that the baby will be born handicapped.
- the pregnancy places existing children under any threat.

TAKE TIME TO THINK

Two doctors must agree on its legality before an abortion can be carried out. It must be carried out before 24 weeks of pregnancy, although there are demands that this time limit should be reduced to 20 or 22 weeks. Most abortions are carried out in the first 12 weeks of pregnancy.

A "*The child, by reason of its physical and mental immaturity, needs special safeguards including legal protection before as well as after birth.*"

United Nations Declaration of Human Rights

ABORTION – THE FACTS

- Before 1967, at least 200,000 abortions were carried out in this country each year illegally. Many women died each year from their injuries. Thousands more were scarred for life or made infertile [unable to have children].
- During 1971, 104,000 abortions were carried out. This figure has now risen to about 160,000 each year. 1 in every 6 pregnancies ends in abortion.
- The largest rise in the number of abortions has been on women in the 16-19 age-group.
- Most abortions are carried out because it is felt that the mental or physical health of the mother would be at risk if the baby was born. Many people complain that this means that few requests for an abortion are rejected – many opponents of abortion call it 'abortion on demand'.

This mother is very excited about the birth of her second baby. What kind of circumstances, however, might lead her to dread the birth of a baby?

WHEN DOES LIFE BEGIN?

In any discussion of abortion, the most important question is 'When does life begin?' There are three possible answers:

- Life begins at the moment when a sperm fertilises the ovum [egg]. This is the moment of conception. This is the view held by Hindus, Jews, Sikhs and many Christians, particularly Roman Catholics. Problem: About 20% of [1 in 5] conceptions end in a miscarriage within weeks of the pregnancy beginning.

- Life begins at some point in the pregnancy. Some religions teach that life begins when God implants a soul in the body. Problem: There is no agreement as to exactly when this happens. Many people do not believe in the soul anyway.

- Life begins either when the baby can survive on its own outside its mother's body [called 'the time of viability'] at about 24 weeks or when it is born. Problem: A baby has all of its organs and is recognisable as a person long before it is born.

OVER TO YOU ▶▶▶

1 What is an abortion?

2 Write down the four conditions under which a legal abortion can be carried out in England and Wales.

3 What has to happen before an abortion can be performed?

4 What kind of special protection do you think a baby should be given – before and after birth?

5 When do you think life begins? What is the opinion of most people in your class?

TAKE TIME TO THINK

In England and Wales, a girl under the age of 16 can obtain an abortion, and advice about contraception, without her parents being informed. Do you think this is right? Look at it from the girl's and from the parents' point of view.

WHAT DO PEOPLE THINK ABOUT ABORTION?

You will find out

- The Pro-Life arguments against abortion.
- The Pro-Choice arguments in favour of abortion.
- The Christian teaching about abortion.

In the glossary

Abortion

Bible

Roman Catholic Church

The rights and wrongs of abortion go to the very heart of religion – is all life sacred and, if so, must it be preserved at all costs? Abortion divides Christians, and non-Christians, into two clearly defined groups:

THE PRO-LIFE CASE

People who are against abortion in all situations are called Pro-Life.

CHECK IT OUT

The Pro-Life argument

Human reasons: All human beings are unique. This includes those who are severely handicapped. These children can live very happy and fulfilled lives. They may only live for a short time and yet they can bring great joy into the lives of others. Everyone has the right to exist.

Adoption: Thousands of couples are infertile and cannot have children. They would love to adopt a baby.

Human rights: Each baby conceived is a potential human being. It has the same right to exist as every other human being. This is why babies need to be protected – both before and after birth. No-one has the right to take that life away.

Find out more:
www.spuc.org.uk
www.lifeuk.org

THE PRO-CHOICE CASE

People who believe that women have the right to choose what happens to their own body are called Pro-Choice.

Find out more: www.abortionrights.org.uk   www.abortion-help.co.uk

A woman's right to choose: Every woman has the right to choose what happens to her own body. To have a baby is an enormous and life-changing decision. If she is not ready, it is better to have an abortion.

Rape: If a woman is pregnant because she has been raped then she must have the right to have an abortion. To have the baby would be a constant reminder of that dreadful event.

The Pro-Choice argument

Personal reasons: If a baby is going to be handicapped then an abortion might be the best way out for everyone. Not everyone can look after a handicapped child for many years. An abortion should always be available if the mother's health or life is at risk.

Social reasons: The family might not be able to afford another child. Abortion should be available for girls under the age of consent – 16.

CHRISTIAN TEACHING ABOUT ABORTION

An early Christian document condemned abortion:

A *"You shall not kill by abortion the fruit of the womb."*

The Bible appears to say that life begins in the mother's womb:

B *"For you created my inmost being; you knit me together in my mother's womb."*

Psalm 139.13

C *"Before I formed you in the womb I knew you; before you were born I set you apart."*

Jeremiah 1.5

None of the Christian Churches believe that abortion should be encouraged and most agree that it should only be used in the most serious of medical circumstances. The Roman Catholic Church believes that it is never justified – not even if the mother's life is in danger or if she has been raped.

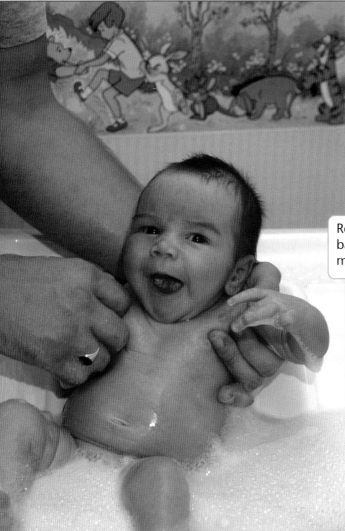

Roman Catholics believe that the life of a baby should be placed above that of the mother if a choice has to be made.

OVER TO YOU ▶▶▶

1. Imagine that you have been asked to present the main arguments against abortion to your class. What would you say to support your argument?
2. Imagine that you have been asked to present a case to support the necessity of having abortion available. What would you say to support your argument?
3. Do you find the arguments against abortion more convincing or vice versa? Give some reasons for reaching your conclusion, whatever it is.

TAKE TIME TO THINK

The decision about abortion takes medical, social and personal considerations into account. No importance, however, is attached to the feelings of the father. Do you think that this is right – or does it simply allow fathers off the hook?

WHAT DO CHRISTIANS BELIEVE ABOUT SEX?

You will find out

- The reasons why sex is such an important part of life.

- The Christian approach to pre-marital and extra-marital sex.

In the glossary

Adultery

Celibacy

Chastity

Roman Catholic Church

Paul

Monk

New Testament

Nun

Priest

WHAT SEX IS ALL ABOUT

Most people agree that sex is a normal, and very important, part of life for almost everyone. What, though, are the reasons why people have sex? What do you think? Here are some of the reasons that have been put forward:

Sex is the way of making sure that the human race survives. No children – no future. Most people will have children at some time and bring them up. Until recently, the vast majority of parents were married although, now, almost as many children are born to couples who cohabit [live together without being married].

Philip

Sex is the best way for two people to express their feelings of love for each other. In sex, two people give themselves totally to each other. Christians believe that sex is a gift from God and this belief is expressed in the Marriage Service.

Yvonne

Some people believe that sex is purely for enjoyment. Love might come into the equation but it doesn't have to. This gives rise to 'one night stands' or 'casual sex' and is something that Christians do not agree with.

Samantha

The Roman Catholic Church is the only Church to insist that its priests remain unmarried and celibate.

WHAT DO CHRISTIANS BELIEVE ABOUT SEX?

A *"I tell you that anyone who looks at a woman lustfully has already committed adultery with her in his heart."*

Matthew 5.28: Jesus

Most Christians believe that:

- Sex is a gift from God.

- Sex should only take place within the security of marriage.

- Sex is given by God so that a couple will be blessed by having children – also a gift from God.

Adultery refers to sexual relations between two people who are not married to each other and one or both of whom are married to someone else. As extract A shows, Jesus not only taught that adultery itself was wrong but also that it was wrong to even have adulterous thoughts. He was really pointing out that one thing can lead to another where sex is concerned.

Because of the advice of Jesus, many Christians believe that they should practise **chastity** outside marriage. This means that a couple do not have any sexual relations until they are married. This is the clear teaching of the Roman Catholic Church [B].

B *"Every sexual act must be within the framework of marriage."*

Roman Catholic Document 'Casti Conubii'

Celibacy is the chosen way of life that excludes marriage and sex. It has been associated with the Roman Catholic Church and its priests for centuries. It was inspired by the example of Paul in the New Testament, who was certainly unmarried. He said that anyone who wished to dedicate themselves to the service of God would best remain celibate. Roman Catholic priests, monks and nuns still follow this advice today.

OVER TO YOU ▶▶▶

1 Think of three reasons why sex is an important human activity. Place them in what you think are their order of importance. Discuss these reasons with your partner.

2 What is your opinion of casual sex?

3 Do you think that Jesus was being realistic in extract A or does everyone have these thoughts sometimes?

TAKE TIME TO THINK

Someone has said that: "A girl plays at sex, for which she is not ready, because what she wants is love; a boy plays at love, for which he is not ready, because what he wants is sex." Explain what you think this person is saying. Do you agree with it?

GROWING OLD

You will find out

- Different opinions about when old age begins.

- Facts and figures about old age in the UK.

- The way that Christians treat old age.

In the glossary

Bible

Church

Heaven

Minister

Priest

Ten Commandments

Most churches do all that they can to help the elderly in their area.

A *"There is a season for everything, a time for every occupation under heaven. A time for giving birth, a time for dying."*

Ecclesiastes 3.1-2

WHAT IS OLD AGE?

Everyone grows old some day. That, of course, is an obvious thing to say but few young people have a clear idea about what it is really like to grow old.

What, though, is old age and when does it begin? Until recently, most people would have said that old age started around the age of 65 – the age at which people become eligible to draw their old age pension.

The idea of 'old age', however, has now been redrawn. Better medical facilities and a higher standard of living means that people are now living much longer. The average life expectancy in the UK is now about 78 years for men and 82 for women. We now know that, by the year 2025, people will be expected to work well beyond their 65th birthday and that is why people now talk of 'old age' beginning at 75.

GROWING OLD – THE FACTS

As we have seen, it is a simple fact of life that men and women in the UK are living much longer than people did 50 years ago. This is not, however, good news all the way:

- 3 out of every 4 people over the age of 65 report that they are living with a major disease or illness.

- People over the age of 70 are seven times more likely to visit their doctor than those who are 30 years old.

- The longer a person lives, the fewer contemporaries [people of the same age] survive to be their friends. In all surveys, loneliness emerges as one of the major problems that elderly people face. 75% of women and 50% of men aged 85 and over live alone. 15% of older people say that they often go a whole week without meeting anyone that they know.

OVER TO **YOU** ▶▶▶

1 Write down ten words which, in your opinion, sum up what it is like to grow old. Here are two words that you might want to include: retired, lonely. Discuss your list with your partner. Do you have similar ideas about the experience of growing old?

2 When do you think old age begins? Give some reasons for your answer.

3 What do you think is the best age to be? Explain your opinion. Do your friends agree with your conclusion?

4 Do you think there are some good points to growing old or is it bad news all the way?

5 Imagine that you are elderly and lonely. What would you like your local church to do for you?

CHRISTIAN RESPONSES

"My son, keep your father's commandment, and forsake not your mother's teaching. When you walk, they will lead you; when you lie down, they will watch over you; and when you wake, they will talk with you. A wise son hears his father's instruction but a scoffer does not listen to rebuke."

Proverbs 20.21

"Christians have their beliefs about life after death to sustain them as they grow older and they hope that they will go to heaven. They are given this assurance in the Bible. The Bible also gives very clear guidance to people about how they should treat their parents, starting with one of the Ten Commandments – "Honour your father and mother.""

Alan, 21

Each church has its own programme for helping older members of the congregation. This might include:

a) Lunch clubs
b) Outings and excursions
c) Social evenings
d) Visits from the priest or minister
e) Arranging transport to church

WHAT IS EUTHANASIA?

You will find out

- What euthanasia means.
- Christian attitudes to euthanasia.
- The arguments for and against euthanasia.

In the glossary

Euthanasia

Hospice

Monk

Roman Catholic Church

The word **euthanasia** comes from two Greek words meaning 'a good death'. It can be used in four different ways:

Active euthanasia: when a lethal injection is given to end a person's life.

Voluntary euthanasia: when someone asks a doctor or loved-one for help to die.

What can euthanasia mean?

Passive euthanasia: when treatment which would keep a person alive is withdrawn.

Involuntary euthanasia: when a person is in a coma and someone else decides that treatment is stopped.

TAKE TIME TO THINK

Here are two real-life situations for you to think about – and discuss:

1. Tony Bland was a football supporter who was crushed in the Hillsborough disaster. He lived in a PVS [Persistent Vegetative State] for many years until his family obtained permission to withdraw his feeding. He died soon afterwards.
2. Diane Pretty suffered from motor neurone disease, a condition that leads to a slow and very painful death. She went to court for permission for her husband to be allowed to help her die. Although permission was refused she soon died naturally.

CHRISTIANS AND EUTHANASIA

Both individual Christians and Churches have very strong feelings about euthanasia:

The Roman Catholic Church is totally opposed to euthanasia [A]:

A   *"Euthanasia is a temptation to take the life of a man under the false pretext of giving them a pleasant and quiet death. This is a crime which cannot become legal by any means."*

Pope Paul VI [1963-78]

Most other Christian Churches are opposed to euthanasia but some are more flexible than others. They will accept, for example, the turning off of a life-support machine in certain situations. Each Church bases its teaching on the belief that life is sacred because everyone is created by God.

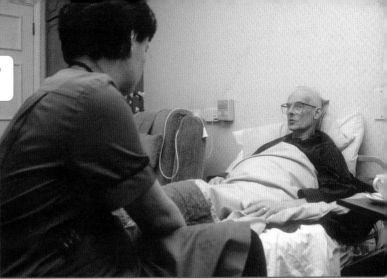

Some people go into a hospice to spend the last days of their lives.

ARGUMENTS FOR EUTHANASIA

* People should not have to suffer unnecessarily.
* Everyone has the right to decide when and how they will die.
* In some situations, helping someone to die may be the most loving thing to do.
* Energy and resources should be concentrated on those who can recover and live.
* Keeping someone alive with drugs when they are very ill is actually going against God's will.
* Euthanasia allows people to die peacefully and with dignity.

ARGUMENTS AGAINST EUTHANASIA

* A sick person may not be able to make a rational decision.
* Doctors might take the easiest way out.
* Life is a gift of God and only he can take it away.
* There are instances of people recovering miraculously against all the odds.
* Suffering can bring some people closer to God.
* Hospices provide people with medical help to cope with great pain.

OVER TO YOU ▶▶▶

1 What are the different ways in which the word 'euthanasia' can be used?

2 Try to explain what you think about euthanasia.

3 What do you think about the two cases of Tony Bland and Diane Pretty?

4 What are the main arguments for and against euthanasia?

THE HOSPICE MOVEMENT

Many Christians believe that the Hospice Movement is the answer to euthanasia. Its roots are found centuries ago when monks offered care for the sick and dying. Recently, hospices have been revived to offer care for those who are dying – a branch of medicine called 'palliative care'. The Hospice Movement is based on the belief that there are now drugs available which can guarantee everyone a comfortable death.

Many hospices have a Christian foundation, although they admit people of all religious beliefs – and none. An important part of hospice care is that nurses have time to spend talking with patients, trying to answer their fears about dying. There are, however, nowhere near enough hospice places to meet the demand.

Dr Cicely Saunders was the founder of the modern Hospice Movement. You can read her comments in extract B.

B   *"All those who work with dying people are anxious that terminal care [looking after the dying] everywhere should become so good that no-one ever need to ask for voluntary euthanasia."*

Dr Saunders

TAKE TIME TO THINK

Do you think that we should spend much more money on hospices so that people can die peacefully? Why do you think that we don't do this?

You will find out

- The teaching of the Bible on the role of women in the Church.

- The attitude of the different Christian Churches towards the role of women.

In the glossary

Altar

Baptist Church

Bible

Church of England

Holy Communion

Methodist Church

Minister

Nonconformist Churches

Paul

Priest

Sin

Jesus lived 2,000 years ago in a society in which men were firmly in control. Some Christians believe that society should still be like this, with men taking the lead and women supporting their husbands and bringing up the children. Other Christians, however, think that this is a very old-fashioned view and out of place in the modern world.

THE BIBLE AND WOMEN

The Christian Church has often been accused of being sexist and prejudiced against women. This is because the Church, from the time of Paul, has been run by men who have followed what they believed to be the teaching of the Bible:

A *"I permit no woman to teach or to have authority over men; she is to keep silent."*

Paul 1. Timothy 2.11-12

B *"Wives should submit to their husbands in everything."*

Paul. Ephesians 5.24

The Church taught that sin entered the world because Eve disobeyed God and gave her husband the fruit to eat. This was believed to be the way that sin entered the world – a disaster for which the woman was mainly to blame!

Here is one example from a later Christian leader which shows how the words of Paul have been interpreted.

C *"Women should remain at home, sit still, keep the house, bear children and bring them up."*

Martin Luther, important Christian leader of the 16th century

WHAT ABOUT WOMEN PRIESTS?

No to women priests: The Roman Catholic and Orthodox Churches have a combined membership of about 1.5 billion. Neither of them allow women to be ordained to be priests. The reasons they give are:

- When the priest stands at the altar to give the bread and wine of Holy Communion, he is representing Christ and a woman cannot do that.

- Jesus chose twelve men to be his disciples. A priest is the spiritual descendant of these original disciples and so cannot be female.

- The Bible says clearly [A] that women are not to preach in church or have any authority over men.

These Christians believe that women should support their husbands in every way – but not try to be their equal. Men and women have different skills and roles to play.

You will find women taking services in some Christian Churches.

Yes to women priests: The Nonconformist Churches, such as the Baptists, the Methodists and the United Reformed Churches, have admitted women ministers for decades. The Church of England has allowed women priests since 1994. They argue that:

- In God's eyes it is totally irrelevant whether a person is male or female. They quote the words of Paul:

D *"There is neither Jew nor Greek, slave nor free, male nor female, for you are all one in Christ Jesus."*

Galatians 3.28

- In many cases, women are more suited to being priests than men – they can be more caring and sympathetic.

- The Church should set an example to the rest of society in showing that it believes in true equality.

- Jesus lived in a very different world to the one found today. You cannot treat women in the same way as they were treated then.

These Churches believe that the dignity of both men and women demand that they are given equal opportunities.

OVER TO **YOU** ▶▶▶

1 Where have some Christians got the idea from that wives should submit themselves to their husbands?

2 Write out, in your own words, two opinions about the part that women should play in the life of the Church.

3 Do you think there is some truth in the belief that men and women bring different skills to life – and they should not try to be the same?

4 Imagine that you have been asked to take part in a debate either arguing for or against allowing women to become priests or ministers in church. Write out the arguments that you would use to underline your case.

5 "A Christian wife is under an obligation to support her husband and do what he says." Do you agree? Give reasons to support your answer, showing that you have thought about more than one point of view.

WHAT IS ISLAMOPHOBIA?

You will find out

- What Islamophobia is.
- How Islamophobia works.
- What can be done about Islamophobia.

In the glossary

Islamophobia

WHAT IS ISLAMOPHOBIA?

It is very important that different religious groups learn to live happily together. Christianity, as the largest religion in the UK, has a special responsibility to work for understanding and tolerance.

Islam is a religion of peace and anti-violence. **Islamophobia** is built on an ignorance of Islam as a religion and the religious life of individual Muslims.

Islamophobia is a fear or hatred of everything connected with the religion of Islam and those who follow this religion. It is the belief that many Muslims:

- are religious fanatics.
- have violent feelings to all non-Muslims.
- reject such ideas as the equality of all men and women and the freedom of all people to worship God as they please.

Two recent events have made Islamophobia much worse both in Britain and overseas:

- The destruction of the Twin Towers in New York in September 2001.
- The bombings on the London Underground system and one bus in July 2005.

> I am a Muslim young person and I am very serious about the teachings of my faith. I believe that my religion is one of peace and I certainly do not believe in using violence. It has, however, become increasingly difficult to convince people of this. People are now very suspicious of me and what I do. Whether I like it or not, many people now see me as dangerous. It seems that this is the way that they will always look at me in future.

Muhammad, 19

Muhammad is talking here of a stereotype [a fixed picture] that some people hold of all those who follow Islam. Because a few people who claim to be Muslims have committed terrible acts of violence in the name of their religion, some people look at all Muslims in this way. As a result, there is much prejudice directed against Muslims as a group and their religious faith.

ISLAMOPHOBIA IN ACTION

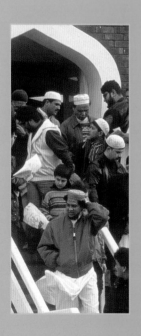

Race attack on imam near mosque in Wales.

Man jailed for anti-Muslim slurs in Cumbria.

Thug jailed for Muslim racism in Cambridge.

In recent years, there have been examples of Islamophobia from countries as far apart as Australia, Spain, Canada, Greece and in many European cities. Muslims have been attacked and abused in a whole succession of unpleasant and violent attacks.

What can be done about it?

People who are working for religious tolerance in Britain and other countries insist that non-Muslims should be asking themselves a series of questions, such as:

- How much do I know about Islam?
- Do I make assumptions about Islam that could easily turn out to be untrue?
- How are Muslims reported in the newspapers and on television? Do they only crop up after some act of violence? Are the good and important things that Muslims do reported as well as the more unfortunate ones?
- How do young people form their ideas about Muslims? Do they simply come from what other people tell them? What other sources might these ideas have?
- Is your thinking about Muslims formed by your family, your friends or what you hear on television or read in newspapers?

Islamophobia will take a very long time to wipe out altogether. Indeed many people doubt whether that could ever happen.

OVER TO YOU ▶▶▶

1   What do you think Islamophobia is and have you come across it?

2   Do you regard the followers of Islam in a different way to the followers of any other religion – or none?

3   Are you a Muslim or do you know many Muslims? Is your opinion of Muslims based upon personal experience or simply on what you have heard on television or read in the newspapers?

4   Can you really imagine how Muhammad feels as a Muslim living in Britain? Have you ever felt like an outsider?

TAKE TIME TO THINK

What kind of society would you like to see as you grow up and have children of your own? Are you optimistic or pessimistic as you look into the future?

GLOSSARY

Abortion: The removal of an embryo from a womb using a surgical procedure.

Absolution: The pronouncement of a priest in the Roman Catholic Church that a person's sins have been forgiven after they have confessed them.

Adultery: Sexual relations between a married person and someone to whom he or she is not married.

Agnostic: A person who is not sure whether God exists or not.

Altar: The raised platform at the front of an Anglican and Roman Catholic church from which the services of Holy Communion and the Mass are conducted.

Anglican Church: A worldwide fellowship of independent churches based on the teachings of the Church of England.

Anointing the Sick: The practice of the priest in the Roman Catholic Church of anointing the forehead of a sick person with consecrated oil.

Archbishop: The two leading priests in the Church of England – the Archbishop of Canterbury and the Archbishop of York.

Ascension: The journey of Jesus into heaven at the end of his life on Earth.

Atheist: A person who does not believe that God exists.

Baptism: The Christian practice of sprinkling water over a baby [Infant Baptism] or immersing adult believers [Believer's Baptism].

Baptist Church: The Protestant Church which believes that all Christians should be baptised as adults.

Beatitudes: The statements by Jesus in the Sermon on the Mount [Matthew 5:7] indicating those who are spiritually happy.

Believer's Baptism: The practice in Baptist churches of baptising adult believers.

Bible: The holy book of Christianity.

Bishop: A priest who has responsibility for the churches in a wide area [called a 'diocese'].

Breaking of Bread: One of the most popular terms for Holy Communion in Nonconformist Churches.

Cardinal: A senior priest in the Roman Catholic Church.

Cathedral: The most important church in a Roman Catholic or Anglican diocese.

Celibacy: The decision by a Roman Catholic priest, monk or nun to live a life without any sexual relationships.

Chapel: Small Nonconformist church.

Chastity: Living a life without any sexual relationships.

Chrismation: The service in the Orthodox Church which combines Infant Baptism with confirmation.

Christmas: Festival which celebrates the birth of Jesus.

Church: The building in which Christians meet for worship.

Church of England: The main Christian Church in the UK.

Citadel: The building in which members of the Salvation Army hold their services.

Cloning: A copy or a replica of a part of the human body or of the complete person, having the same DNA.

Confession: Practice of Roman Catholics of confessing their sins to a priest so that they can receive God's forgiveness.

Confirmation: The service held by the Roman Catholic and Anglican Churches in which people 'confirm' the vows that were taken for them when they were baptised.

Conscience: The faculty which Christians believe to be the voice of God telling them how they should behave.

Creed: An ancient statement of belief recited in many Roman Catholic, Orthodox and Anglican services.

Cross: The universally recognised symbol of the Christian faith.

Crucifix: A cross holding the figure of Jesus either worn around the neck or found in a church.

Developed World: The rich countries in the world.

Developing World: The poor countries in the world.

Diocese: An area of the country over which a Church of England bishop has leadership of the churches.

Divine Liturgy: The name given to the service of Holy Communion in the Orthodox Church.

Easter: The Christian festival at which the death and resurrection of Jesus are remembered and celebrated.

Embryo: A baby in its earliest stages of development in the womb.

Eucharist: The name given in many Anglican churches to the celebration of Holy Communion.

Euthanasia: The ending of someone's life early because they are suffering from an incurable illness.

Evangelical: A large group of Christians from many denominations who believe in the truth of the Bible and in personal conversion.

Evolution: The scientific theory which maintains that human beings are descended from other forms of life.

Font: The receptacle in a church that holds the water used in the service of Infant Baptism.

Free Churches: Churches such as the Baptist and Methodist which do not accept the leadership of the Roman Catholic or Anglican Churches, also called Nonconformist Churches.

Free Will: The freedom which Christians believe that everyone has to choose whether to accept God in their lives or not.

Genetic Engineering: Controlling genetic defects by modifying or eliminating certain genes during pregnancy.

Gospel: One of four books in the New Testament which record the life and the teachings of Jesus.

Gurdwara: The building in which Sikhs meet for worship.

Heaven: The place which is believed by Christians to be the destination of those who believe in God and Jesus.

Hell: The place which is believed by many Christians to be the destination of the wicked.

Holy Communion: One of the most popular names for the service at which Christians eat bread and drink wine to remember and celebrate the death and Resurrection of Jesus.

Holy Spirit: The third member of the Trinity in Christian belief along with God the Father and Jesus.

Hospice: A hospital that practises palliative medicine, offering pain control during the last few days of life.

HIV: Human Immunodeficiency Virus.

Humanist: A person who believes that human beings must face life without the help of a nonexistent God.

Icon: A special religious painting showing Jesus or the Holy Family, used by Orthodox Christians in their devotions.

GLOSSARY

Incarnation: God becoming a human being, the word used to describe the life of Jesus on Earth.

Infant Baptism: The practice of the Roman Catholic and Anglican Churches in baptising babies.

Islamophobia: A fear of everything to do with the religion of Islam.

Just War: The belief of some Christians that a war can be justified if it is fought according to certain rules.

Lectern: The stand on which a Bible is placed in a church.

Lord's Prayer: The prayer that Jesus taught his followers to use, used in many church services.

Lord's Supper: A favourite term used in many Nonconformist Churches for the service of Holy Communion.

Mass: The term used by the Roman Catholic Church for the service of Holy Communion.

Meeting House: A Quaker place of worship.

Methodist Church: One of the most important Nonconformist Churches.

Minister: The man or woman who leads the worship in a Nonconformist Church.

Miracle: An event which seems to have no natural explanation.

Monk: A man who dedicates himself to God and lives a celibate life in a monastery.

New Testament: The second part of the Bible, containing the four Gospels and letters by early Church leaders.

Nonconformist Church: A church which does not belong to the Roman Catholic, Anglican or Orthodox Churches.

Nun: A woman who dedicates herself to God by living a celibate life and living in a convent.

Old Testament: The first part of the Bible, contains the same books as the Jewish Scriptures.

Ordination: The services in the Roman Catholic and Anglican churches which dedicates people to the service of the church.

Orthodox Church: One of the three great Churches together with the Roman Catholic and Anglican Churches.

Pacifism: The belief held by many Christians, and others, that the use of violence is never justified.

Parable: Story told by Jesus which had a moral or spiritual lesson.

Paul: Early leader of the Christian Church, writer of many letters in the New Testament.

Pentecostal Church: One of the Nonconformist Churches.

Peter: Most prominent disciple of Jesus, believed by Catholics to have been the first Pope.

Pope: The spiritual leader of the Roman Catholic Church.

Priest: A person who is ordained in the Roman Catholic or Anglican Churches and so is authorised to take services.

Prophet: A man or a woman who is sent to deliver a message by God.

Protestant Church: Includes Churches which are not Roman Catholic or Orthodox.

Pulpit: A raised platform in a church from which the sermon is given.

Purgatory: The place which Catholics believe to be in between Earth and heaven, a place of cleansing for the soul before it reaches heaven.

Quakers: One of the smaller Christian Churches, noticeable for its belief in pacifism.

Refugee: Someone who has lost their home and country, usually as the result of a war.

Resurrection: The belief that God brought Jesus back from the dead, the most important Christian belief.

Roman Catholic Church: The largest of the Christian Churches, led by the Pope.

Sabbath Day: The Jewish holy day.

Sacrament: Special services in the Roman Catholic, Orthodox and Anglican Churches believed to dispense God's special blessing.

Saint: A Christian man or woman particularly noted for the holiness of their life.

Salvation Army: A Nonconformist Church most notable for its distinctive uniform and social work in the community.

Satan: The force of evil in Christian belief who fights a constant battle against the goodness of God.

Sermon: The part in a service where an extract from the Bible is explained to the congregation.

Sin: An act which is against the will of God.

Soul: The spiritual part of a person that is capable of worshipping God.

Steward: Human beings who are given the responsibility of looking after the planet by God.

Synagogue: The building in which Jews meet for worship.

Ten Commandments: Very important laws given to the Jewish people during their journey out of slavery in Egypt.

Theist: Someone who believes in God.

Transubstantiation: The belief of Roman Catholics that the bread and wine become the actual body and blood of Jesus during the Mass.

Trinity: The Christian belief that God makes himself known in three forms – as God the Father, God the Son and God the Holy Spirit.

Vegan: Someone who does not eat meat or any meat products.

Vegetarian: Someone who does not eat meat.

Viaticum: The last Communion given to a Roman Catholic before he or she dies.

Vicar: A man or a woman in the Church of England who leads the services.

Virgin Mary: The mother of Jesus, highly honoured by Roman Catholics.

Vivisection: The use of animals in scientific experiments.

Vocation: A calling, used to describe the way that a priest understands his or her future work.

Xenotransplantation: Transplanting animal organs into human beings.

Badger Publishing Limited
15 Wedgwood Gate
Pin Green Industrial Estate
Stevenage, Hertfordshire SG1 4SU
Telephone: 01438 356907
Fax: 01438 747015
www.badger-publishing.co.uk
enquiries@badger-publishing.co.uk

Badger KS3 Religious Education
Christian Beliefs and Issues

First published 2007
ISBN 978-1-84691-084-5

Acknowledgements
   Photos © Alex Keene, The Walking Camera, with the following exceptions:
   Tsunami p.5, Vivisection p.87 © Sipa Press / **Rex Features**.
   Darwin p.51 © Popperfoto, Embryo p.54 © Medical-on-Line, Amnesty International
   p.64 © Kathy deWitt, AIDs clinic p.77 © Photo Network / **Alamy**.
   Dolly p.53, Protest p.56, Transplant patient p.59, War pp.90-91,
   Flood p.101 © **EMPICS**.
   Satan p.61 from Theophilus selling his soul © Lincoln Cathedral, reproduced with kind permission. With thanks to Tom Küpper.
   Baby Anna p.68 © Elena Wilmott.
   Tearfund p.74 © Jim Loring/Tearfund – used by permission (www.tearfund.org). With thanks to Margaret Chandler.
   Children p.83 © Arthur Tilley, Hens p.86 © Gary John Norman, Garden p.89 © Kevin Morris, Stone; Atom bomb p.97 © Hulton Archive / **Getty Images**.
   Religions for Peace pp.98-99 reproduced with kind permission from Religions for Peace, with thanks to Andrea Louie.
   Granny Joy p.117 © Paul Martin Digital.

Publisher: David Jamieson
Editor: Paul Martin
Designer: Adam Wilmott
Illustrator: Juliet Breese (p.12)
Cover photo: Alex Keene

Printed in Hong Kong through Colorcraft Ltd.,Hong Kong